TITLES AND FORMS

OF ADDRESS

a Guide to Correct Use

Twenty-third edition

A&C Black
An Imprint of Bloomsbury Publishing Plc

BLOOMSBURY

LONDON • OXFORD • NEW YORK • NEW DELHI • SYDNEY

www.bloomsbury.com

50 Bedford Square   1385 Broadway
London   New York
WC1B 3DP   NY 10018
UK   USA

First edition 1918	Twelfth edition 1964
Second edition 1929	Thirteenth edition 1968
Third edition 1932	Fourteenth edition 1971
Fourth edition 1936	Fifteenth edition 1976
Fifth edition 1939	Sixteenth edition 1978
Sixth edition 1945	Seventeenth edition 1980
Seventh edition 1949	Eighteenth edition 1985
Eighth edition 1951	Nineteenth edition 1990
Ninth edition 1955	Twentieth edition 1997
Tenth edition 1958	Twenty-first edition 2002
Eleventh edition 1961	Twenty-second edition 2007

A&C BLACK and the 'WHO'S WHO PUBLISHED ANNUALLY SINCE 1849'
belt logo are trademarks of Bloomsbury Publishing Plc

British Library Cataloguing-in-Publication Data
A catalogue record for this book is available from the British Library.

ISBN: HB: 978-1-472-92433-9

2 4 6 8 10 9 7 5 3 1

Printed and bound in Great Britain by
CPI Group (UK) Ltd, Croydon, CR0 4YY

To find out more about our authors and books visit www.bloomsbury.com.
Here you will find extracts, author interviews, details of forthcoming events
and the option to sign up for our newsletters.

FOREWORD

The correct use of titles, and other distinguishing marks of honour or of office, has generally become established over a long period through the usage followed by the title-holders themselves and by those associated with them. Similarly, and very gradually, there occur modifications and changes in practice.

It seems desirable to point out that while great formality may from time to time be appropriate, and the forms to be used in such cases are therefore given, it will more often be proper – and more usual – to use simpler forms, as indicated throughout, in ordinary correspondence whether business or social, especially if e-mail is the mode employed rather than traditional letter-writing. The forms are even more relaxed when using social media.

In view of security risks, it is wise to enquire in advance how envelopes should be addressed to people at home. If that is not possible, omit title, office and rank, unless advised otherwise by the recipient. This precaution obviously relates particularly to members of the armed forces, the police and legal officers (from judges to members of the prison service).

It should be made clear that etiquette is a different subject and is not touched upon in this book.

The publishers are grateful to correspondents who have kindly suggested additions and improvements. At the same time they are bound to say that they are unable to provide an advisory or information service.

2016

Contents

Contents

THE PEERAGE: Barons and Baronesses 43

THE BARONETAGE 48

KNIGHTS AND DAMES 52

THE ARMED FORCES: Royal Air Force 116

LAW, DIPLOMATIC AND GOVERNMENT 120

HONOURS, QUALIFICATIONS AND APPOINTMENTS 149

REPLYING FORMALLY TO FORMAL INVITATIONS 155

SOME PRONUNCIATIONS OF PROPER NAMES 157

ORDER OF PRECEDENCE 184

INDEX 189

ABBREVIATIONS

This list consists solely of abbreviations which may be used after the name. These fall into two groups:

- they require forms of address described in the text of this book;
- they are fellowships or similar qualifications which would be used only in a professional context.

Pages 149–154 give the rules by which the order of the various categories is determined.

The selection is restricted to the above two groups because so many initials and acronyms are now in use. For fuller and more comprehensive information readers are referred to:

Who's Who

Published annually by A & C Black

A

AA	Augustinians of the Assumption
AB	Bachelor of Arts (US)
AC	Companion, Order of Australia
AD	Dame of the Order of Australia
ADC	Aide-de-camp
AE	Air Efficiency Award
AEM	Air Efficiency Medal
AFC	Air Force Cross
AFM	Air Force Medal
AK	Knight of the Order of Australia
AM	Albert Medal; Member of the Order of Australia; Master of Arts (US)
AO	Officer of the Order of Australia
AOE	Alberta Order of Excellence
ARA	Associate, Royal Academy
ARRC	Associate, Royal Red Cross

B

BA	Bachelor of Arts
Bart or **Bt**	Baronet
BCL	Bachelor of Civil Law
BD	Bachelor of Divinity
BEM	British Empire Medal
BLitt	Bachelor of Letters
BM	Bachelor of Medicine
BMus	Bachelor of Music
BSc	Bachelor of Science
BSM	Barbados Service Medal
BSS	Barbados Service Star; Bachelor of Science (Social Science)
Bt	Baronet
Btss	Baronetess

C

CA	Chartered Accountant (Scotland and Canada)
CB	Companion, Order of the Bath
CBE	Commander, Order of the British Empire
CBiol	Chartered Biologist
CC	Companion, Order of Canada

CChem	Chartered Chemist
CD	Canadian Forces Decoration; Commander, Order of Distinction (Jamaica)
CEng	Chartered Engineer
CF	Chaplain to the Forces; Companion, Order of Fiji
CGA	Community of the Glorious Ascension
CGM	Conspicuous Gallantry Medal
CH	Companion of Honour
CHB	Companion of Honour of Barbados
ChB	Bachelor of Surgery
CI	Imperial Order of the Crown of India
CIE	Companion, Order of the Indian Empire
CJM	Congregation of Jesus and Mary (Eudist Fathers)
CM	Member, Order of Canada; Congregation of the Mission (Vincentians); Master in Surgery; Certificated Master
CMG	Companion, Order of St Michael and St George
CMM	Commander, Order of Military Merit (Canada)
CNZM	Companion, Order of Merit (NZ)
CPA	Chartered Patent Agent
CPhys	Chartered Physicist
CPM	Colonial Police Medal
CPsychol	Chartered Psychologist
CQ	Chevalier, National Order of Quebec
CR	Community of the Resurrection
CSC	Conspicuous Service Cross; Congregation of the Holy Cross
CSI	Companion, Order of the Star of India; Cross, Order of Solomon Islands
CSSp	Holy Ghost Father
CSSR	Congregation of the Most Holy Redeemer (Redemptorist Order)
CText	Chartered Textile Technologist
CV	Cross of Valour (Canada)
CVO	Commander, Royal Victorian Order

D

DA	Dame of St Andrew, Order of Barbados; Doctor of Arts
DAgr	Doctor of Agriculture
DAppSc	Doctor of Applied Science
Dart	Doctor of Art
DASc	Doctor in Agricultural Sciences

DBA	Doctor of Business Administration
DBE	Dame Commander, Order of the British Empire
Dbus	Doctor of Business
DCB	Dame Commander, Order of the Bath
DCh	Doctor of Surgery
DCL	Doctor of Civil Law; Doctor of Canon Law
DCM	Distinguished Conduct Medal
DCMG	Dame Commander, Order of St Michael and St George
DCN	Dame Commander, Order of the Nation (Antigua and Barbuda)
DCnL	Doctor of Canon Law
DCS	Doctor of Commercial Sciences
DCVO	Dame Commander, Royal Victorian Order
DD	Doctor of Divinity
DDS	Doctor of Dental Surgery
DDSc	Doctor of Dental Science
DE	Doctor of Engineering
DEc or **DEcon**	Doctor of Economics
DEconSc	Doctor of Economic Science
DEd	Doctor of Education
DEng	Doctor of Engineering
DFA	Doctor of Fine Arts
DFC	Distinguished Flying Cross
DFM	Distinguished Flying Medal
DHL	Doctor of Humane Letters; Doctor of Hebrew Literature
DHum	Doctor of Humanities
DHumLit	Doctor of Humane Letters
DJur	*Doctor Juris* (Doctor of Law)
DL	Deputy Lieutenant
DLit or **DLitt**	Doctor of Literature; Doctor of Letters
DM or **DMed**	Doctor of Medicine
DMet	Doctor of Metallurgy
DMus	Doctor of Music
DNZM	Dame Companion, New Zealand Order of Merit
DO	Doctor of Osteopathy
DPh or **DPhil**	Doctor of Philosophy
DeŒcPol	*Doctor Œconomiæ Politicæ* (Doctor of Political Economy)
DSC	Distinguished Service Cross
DSc	Doctor of Science
DScMil	Doctor of Military Science

DSM	Distinguished Service Medal
DSO	Companion of the Distinguished Service Order
DSocSc	Doctor of Social Science
DStJ	Dame of Grace, Most Venerable Order of the Hospital of St John of Jerusalem; Dame of Justice, Most Venerable Order of the Hospital of St John of Jerusalem
DTech	Doctor of Technology
DTh or **DTheol**	Doctor of Theology
DThMin	Doctor of Theology and Ministry
DVM or **DVetMed**	Doctor of Veterinary Medicine
DVMS or **DVM&S**	Doctor of Veterinary Medicine and Surgery
DVSc	Doctor of Veterinary Science

E

ED	Efficiency Decoration; Doctor of Engineering (US)
EdB	Bachelor of Education
EdD	Doctor of Education
EM	Edward Medal; Earl Marshal
ERD	Emergency Reserve Decoration (Army)
Esq.	Esquire
Eur Ing	European Engineer

F

FAcSS	Fellow, Academy of Social Sciences
FAMS	Fellow, Ancient Monuments Society
FArborA	Fellow, Arboricultural Association
FAS	Fellow, Antiquarian Society
FASI	Fellow, Architects' and Surveyors' Institute
FBA	Fellow, British Academy
FBAM	Fellow, British Academy of Management
FBC	Fellow, Birmingham Conservatoire
FBCS	Fellow, British Computer Society
FBHI	Fellow, British Horological Institute
FBHS	Fellow, British Horse Society
FBID	Fellow, British Institute of Interior Design
FBIIBA	Fellow, British Insurance and Investment Brokers' Association
FBIPP	Fellow, British Institute of Professional Photography
FBIR	Fellow, British Institute of Radiology

FBIRA	Fellow, British Institute of Regulatory Affairs
FBIS	Fellow, British Interplanetary Society
FBKSTS	Fellow, British Kinematograph, Sound and Television Society
FBOA	Fellow, British Optical Association
FBOU	Fellow, British Ornithologists' Union
FBPhS	Fellow, British Pharmacological Society
FBPsS	Fellow, British Psychological Society
FBTS	Fellow, British Toxicology Society
FCA	Fellow, Institute of Chartered Accountants
FCAI	Fellow, Royal Anthropological Institute of Great Britain & Ireland
FCAM	Fellow, CAM Foundation
FCBSI	Fellow, Chartered Building Societies Institute (merged with Chartered Institute of Bankers)
FCCA	Fellow, Chartered Association of Certified Accountants
FCCEA	Fellow, Commonwealth Council for Educational Administration
FCCS	Fellow, Corporation of Secretaries
FCFI	Fellow, Clothing and Footwear Institute
FCGI	Fellow, City and Guilds of London Institute
FChS	Fellow, Society of Chiropodists
FCI	Fellow, Institute of Commerce
FCIA	Fellow, Corporation of Insurance Agents
FCIArb	Fellow, Chartered Institute of Arbitrators
FCIB	Fellow, Corporation of Insurance Brokers; Fellow, Chartered Institute of Bankers
FCIBS	Fellow, Chartered Institute of Bankers in Scotland
FCIBSE	Fellow, Chartered Institution of Building Services Engineers
FCIEEM	Fellow, Chartered Institute of Ecology and Environmental Management
FCIH	Fellow, Chartered Institute of Housing
FCIHort	Fellow, Chartered Institute of Horticulture
FCIHT	Fellow, Chartered Institution of Highways & Transportation
FCII	Fellow, Chartered Insurance Institute
FCIJ	Fellow, Chartered Institute of Journalists
FCIL	Fellow, Chartered Institute of Linguists
FCILT	Chartered Fellow, Chartered Institute of Logistics and Transport
FCIM	Fellow, Chartered Institute of Marketing

FCInstCES	Fellow, Chartered Institution of Civil Engineering Surveyors
FCIOB	Fellow, Chartered Institute of Building
FCIPD	Fellow, Chartered Institute of Personnel and Development
FCIPHE	Fellow, Chartered Institute of Plumbing and Heating Engineering
FCIPR	Fellow, Chartered Institute of Public Relations
FCIS	Fellow, Institute of Chartered Secretaries and Administrators
FCILT	Chartered Fellow, Chartered Institute of Logistics and Transport
FCIPS	Fellow, Chartered Institute of Purchasing and Supply
FCIWEM	Fellow, Chartered Institution of Water and Environmental Management
FCLIP	Fellow, Chartered Institute of Library and Information Professionals
FCMA	Fellow, Chartered Institute of Management Accountants (*formerly* Institute of Cost and Management Accountants); Fellow, Communications Management Association
FCMC	Fellow grade, Certified Management Consultant
FCOptom	Fellow, College of Optometrists
FCOT	Fellow, College of Teachers
FCP	Fellow, College of Preceptors
FCPS	Fellow, College of Physicians and Surgeons
FCQI	Fellow, Chartered Quality Institute
FCSD	Fellow, Chartered Society of Designers
FCSI	Fellow, Chartered Institute for Securities & Investment
FCSP	Fellow, Chartered Society of Physiotherapy
FCT	Fellow, Association of Corporate Treasurers; Fellow, College of Teachers
FCTB	Fellow, College of Teachers of the Blind
FDS	Fellow in Dental Surgery
FDSRCPSGlas	Fellow in Dental Surgery, Royal College of Physicians and Surgeons of Glasgow
FDSRCS or **FDS RCS**	Fellow in Dental Surgery, Royal College of Surgeons of England
FDSRCSE	Fellow in Dental Surgery, Royal College of Surgeons of Edinburgh
FEI	Fellow, Energy Institute
FEIS	Fellow, Educational Institute of Scotland

FES	Fellow, Entomological Society; Fellow, Ethnological Society
FFA	Fellow, Faculty of Actuaries (in Scotland); Fellow, Institute of Financial Accountants
FFB	Fellow, Faculty of Building
FFDRCSI	Fellow, Faculty of Dentistry, Royal College of Surgeons in Ireland
FFHom	Fellow, Faculty of Homeopathy
FFOM	Fellow, Faculty of Occupational Medicine
FFPath, RCPI	Fellow, Faculty of Pathologists of the Royal College of Physicians of Ireland
FFPH	Fellow, Faculty of Public Health
FFSRH	Fellow, Faculty of Sexual and Reproductive Healthcare of the Royal College of Obstetricians and Gynaecologists
FGA	Fellow, Gemmological Association
FGCM	Fellow, Guild of Church Musicians
FGE	Fellow, Guild of Glass Engravers
FGI	Fellow, Institute of Certificated Grocers
FGS	Fellow, Geological Society; Fellow, Guildhall School of Music and Drama
FGSM(MT)	Fellow, Guildhall School of Music and Drama (Music Therapy)
FHAS	Fellow, Highland and Agricultural Society of Scotland
FHEA	Fellow, Higher Education Academy
FHS	Fellow, Heraldry Society
FIA	Fellow, Institute and Faculty of Actuaries (formerly Institute of Actuaries)
FIAgrE	Fellow, Institution of Agricultural Engineers
FIAL	Fellow, International Institute of Arts and Letters
FIAM	Fellow, International Academy of Management
FInstAM	Fellow, Institute of Administrative Management
FIAP	Fellow, Institution of Analysts and Programmers
FIAWS	Fellow, International Academy of Wood Science
FIBiotech	Fellow, Institute for Biotechnical Studies
FIBMS	Fellow, Institute of Biomedical Sciences
FIC	Fellow, Imperial College; Fellow, Institute of Consulting
FICAI	Fellow, Institute of Chartered Accountants in Ireland
FICD	Fellow, Institute of Civil Defence; Fellow, International College of Dentists
FICE	Fellow, Institution of Civil Engineers
FICFor	Fellow, Institute of Chartered Foresters
FIChemE	Fellow, Institution of Chemical Engineers

FICI	Fellow, Institute of Chemistry of Ireland
FICM	Fellow, Institute of Credit Management
FICMA	Fellow, Institute of Cost and Management Accountants
FICorr	Fellow, Institute of Corrosion
FICS	Fellow, Institute of Chartered Shipbrokers; Fellow, International College of Surgeons
FICT	Fellow, Institute of Concrete Technology
FICW	Fellow, Institute of Clerks of Works of Great Britain
FIDE	Fellow, Institute of Design Engineers
FIED	Fellow, Institution of Engineering Designers
FIET	Fellow, Institution of Engineering and Technology
FIEx	Fellow, Institute of Export
FIExpE	Fellow, Institute of Explosives Engineers
FIFM	Fellow, Institute of Fisheries Management
FIFP	Fellow, Institute of Freight Professionals
FIFST	Fellow, Institute of Food Science and Technology
FIGCM	Fellow, Incorporated Guild of Church Musicians
FIGD	Fellow, Institute of Grocery Distribution
FIGEM	Fellow, Institution of Gas Engineers and Managers
FIH	Fellow, Institute of the Horse; Fellow, Institute of Hospitality
FIHE	Fellow, Institute of Health Education
FIHospE	Fellow, Institute of Hospital Engineering
FIIC	Fellow, International Institute for Conservation of Historic and Artistic Works
FIIM	Fellow, Institution of Industrial Managers
FIMA	Fellow, Institute of Mathematics and its Applications
FIMarEST	Fellow, Institute of Marine Engineering, Science and Technology
FIMechE	Fellow, Institution of Mechanical Engineers
FIMFT	Fellow, Institute of Maxillo-facial Technology
FIMH	Fellow, Institute of Military History
FIMI	Fellow, Institute of the Motor Industry
FIMIT	Fellow, Institute of Musical Instrument Technology
FIMMM	Fellow, Institute of Materials, Minerals and Mining
FIMS	Fellow, Institute of Mathematical Statistics
FInstAM	Fellow, Institute of Administrative Management
FInstD	Fellow, Institute of Directors
FInstLEx	Fellow, Institute of Legal Executives
FInstM	Fellow, Institute of Meat
FInstMC	Fellow, Institute of Measurement and Control

FInstP	Fellow, Institute of Physics
FInstPI	Fellow, Institute of Patentees and Inventors
FInstRE	Fellow, Institution of Royal Engineers
FInstSMM	Fellow, Institute of Sales and Marketing Management
FIOA	Fellow, Institute of Acoustics
FIPA	Fellow, Institute of Practitioners in Advertising; Fellow, Insolvency Practitioners Association
FIPG	Fellow, Institute of Professional Goldsmiths
FIP3	Fellow, Institute of Paper, Printing and Publishing
FIQ	Fellow, Institute of Quarrying
FIRSE	Fellow, Institute of Railway Signalling Engineers
FIRTE	Fellow, Institute of Road Transport Engineers
FIS	Fellow, Institute of Statisticians
FISA	Fellow, Incorporated Secretaries' Association
FISE	Fellow, Institution of Sales Engineers; Fellow, Institution of Sanitary Engineers
FIST	Fellow, Institute of Science Technology
FISTC	Fellow, Institute of Scientific and Technical Communicators
FIStructE	Fellow, Institution of Structural Engineers
FITE	Fellow, Institution of Electrical and Electronics Technician Engineers
FIWSc	Fellow, Institute of Wood Science
FKC	Fellow, King's College London
FKCHMS	Fellow, King's College Hospital Medical School
FLAI	Fellow, Library Association of Ireland
FLCM	Fellow, London College of Music
FLI	Fellow, Landscape Institute
FLIA	Fellow, Life Insurance Association
FLS	Fellow, Linnean Society
FLSW	Fellow, Learned Society of Wales
FMA	Fellow, Museums Association
FMES	Fellow, Minerals Engineering Society
FMS	Fellow, Institute of Management Services; Fellow, Medical Society
FNAEA	Fellow, National Association of Estate Agents
FNECInst	Fellow, North East Coast Institution of Engineers and Shipbuilders
FNI	Fellow, Nautical Institute
FNucI	Fellow, Nuclear Institute
FOR	Fellowship of Operational Research
FPhS	Fellow, Philosophical Society of England

FPMI	Fellow, Pensions Management Institute
FPhysS	Fellow, Physical Society
FRA	Fellow, Royal Academy
FRAD	Fellow, Royal Academy of Dancing
FRAeS	Fellow, Royal Aeronautical Society
FRAgS	Fellow, Royal Agricultural Societies (*ie* of England, Scotland and Wales)
FRAI	Fellow, Royal Anthropological Institute of Great Britain & Ireland
FRAM	Fellow, Royal Academy of Music
FRAS	Fellow, Royal Astronomical Society; Fellow, Royal Asiatic Society
FRASE	Fellow, Royal Agricultural Society of England
FRBS	Fellow, Royal Society of British Sculptors; Fellow, Royal Botanic Society
FRCA	Fellow, Royal College of Art; Fellow, Royal College of Anaesthetists
FRCEM	Fellow, Royal College of Emergency Medicine
FRCGP	Fellow, Royal College of General Practitioners
FRCM	Fellow, Royal College of Music
FRCN	Fellow, Royal College of Nursing
FRCO	Fellow, Royal College of Organists
FRCO(CHM)	Fellow, Royal College of Organists with Diploma in Choir Training
FRCOG	Fellow, Royal College of Obstetricians and Gynaecologists
FRCOphth	Fellow, Royal College of Ophthalmologists
FRCP	Fellow, Royal College of Physicians, London
FRCPath	Fellow, Royal College of Pathologists
FRCPCH	Fellow, Royal College of Paediatrics and Child Health
FRCPE or **FRCPEd**	Fellow, Royal College of Physicians, Edinburgh
FRCPGlas	Fellow, Royal College of Physicians and Surgeons of Glasgow
FRCPI	Fellow, Royal College of Physicians of Ireland
FRCPsych	Fellow, Royal College of Psychiatrists
FRCR	Fellow, Royal College of Radiologists
FRCS	Fellow, Royal College of Surgeons of England
FRCSE or **FRCSEd**	Fellow, Royal College of Surgeons of Edinburgh
FRCSGlas	Fellow, Royal College of Physicians and Surgeons of Glasgow

FRCSI	Fellow, Royal College of Surgeons in Ireland
FRCSLT	Fellow, Royal College of Speech and Language Therapists
FRCSoc	Fellow, Royal Commonwealth Society
FRCS (OMFS)	Fellow, Royal College of Surgeons of England (Oral and Maxillofacial Surgery)
FRCVS	Fellow, Royal College of Veterinary Surgeons
FREconS	Fellow, Royal Economic Society
FREng	Fellow, Royal Academy of Engineering
FRES	Fellow, Royal Entomological Society of London
FRGS	Fellow, Royal Geographical Society
FRHistS	Fellow, Royal Historical Society
FRI	Fellow, Royal Institution
FRIAS	Fellow, Royal Incorporation of Architects of Scotland
FRIBA	Fellow, Royal Institute of British Architects (*and see* RIBA)
FRICS	Fellow, Royal Institution of Chartered Surveyors
FRIN	Fellow, Royal Institute of Navigation
FRINA	Fellow, Royal Institution of Naval Architects
FRMCM	Fellow, Royal Manchester College of Music
FRMedSoc	Fellow, Royal Medical Society
FRMetS	Fellow, Royal Meteorological Society
FRMS	Fellow, Royal Microscopical Society
FRNCM	Fellow, Royal Northern College of Music
FRNS	Fellow, Royal Numismatic Society
FRPharmS	Fellow, Royal Pharmaceutical Society
FRPS	Fellow, Royal Photographic Society
FRPSL	Fellow, Royal Philatelic Society, London
FRS	Fellow, Royal Society
FRSAI	Fellow, Royal Society of Antiquaries of Ireland
FRSAMD	Fellow, Royal Scottish Academy of Music and Drama
FRSB	Fellow, Royal Society of Biology
FRSC	Fellow, Royal Society of Canada; Fellow, Royal Society of Chemistry
FRSCM	Hon. Fellow, Royal School of Church Music
FRSE	Fellow, Royal Society of Edinburgh
FRSGS	Fellow, Royal Scottish Geographical Society
FRSL	Fellow, Royal Society of Literature
FRSM	Fellow, Royal Schools of Music
FRSPH	Fellow, Royal Society for Public Health
FRSTM&H	Fellow, Royal Society of Tropical Medicine and Hygiene

FRTPI	Fellow, Royal Town Planning Institute
FRTS	Fellow, Royal Television Society
FRVC	Fellow, Royal Veterinary College
FRZSScot	Fellow, Royal Zoological Society of Scotland
FSA	Fellow, Society of Antiquaries
FSAE	Fellow, Society of Automotive Engineers; Fellow, Society of Art Education
FSAScot	Fellow, Society of Antiquaries of Scotland
FSCA	Fellow, Society of Company and Commercial Accountants
FSDC	Fellow, Society of Dyers and Colourists
FSE	Fellow, Society of Engineers
FSG	Fellow, Society of Genealogists
FSGT	Fellow, Society of Glass Technology
FSLTC	Fellow, Society of Leather Technologists and Chemists
FSRHE	Fellow, Society for Research into Higher Education
FSS	Fellow, Royal Statistical Society
FSTD	Fellow, Society of Typographic Designers
FTCD	Fellow, Trinity College, Dublin
FTCL	Fellow, Trinity College of Music, London
FTI	Fellow, Textile Institute
FTII	Fellow, Chartered Institute of Taxation
FWA	Fellow, World Academy of Art and Science
FWeldI	Fellow, Welding Institute
FZS	Fellow, Zoological Society

G

GBE	Knight or Dame Grand Cross, Order of the British Empire
GC	George Cross
GCB	Knight or Dame Grand Cross, Order of the Bath
GCIE	Knight Grand Commander, Order of the Indian Empire
GCM	Gold Crown of Merit (Barbados)
GCMG	Knight or Dame Grand Cross, Order of St Michael and St George
GCMJ	Knight or Dame Grand Cross, Supreme Military Order of the Temple of Jerusalem
GCSG	Knight Grand Cross, Order of St Gregory the Great
GCStJ	Bailiff or Dame Grand Cross, Most Venerable Order of the Hospital of St John of Jerusalem
GCSI	Knight Grand Commander, Order of the Star of India

GCVO	Knight or Dame Grand Cross, Royal Victorian Order
GM	George Medal
GNZM	Knight Grand Companion, New Zealand Order of Merit
GOQ	Grand Officier, National Order of Quebec (Canada)

H

HM	His (or Her) Majesty, or Majesty's

I

IRRV	(Fellow/Member of) Institute of Revenues, Rating and Valuation
ISO	Imperial Service Order

J

JCD	*Juris Canonici* (or *Civilis*) *Doctor* (Doctor of Canon (or Civil) Law)
Jnr	Junior
JP	Justice of the Peace
JSD	Doctor of Juristic Science

K

KA	Knight (or Dame) of St Andrew, Order of Barbados
KBE	Knight Commander, Order of the British Empire
KC	King's Counsel
KCB	Knight Commander, Order of the Bath
KCIE	Knight Commander, Order of the Indian Empire
KCMG	Knight Commander, Order of St Michael and St George
KCN	Knight Commander, Order of the Nation (Antigua and Barbuda)
KCSI	Knight Commander, Order of the Star of India
KCVO	Knight Commander, Royal Victorian Order
KG	Knight, Order of the Garter
KGCN	Knight Grand Cross, Order of the Nation (Antigua and Barbuda)
KGN	Knight Grand Collar, Order of the Nation (Antigua and Barbuda)
KHC	Hon. Chaplain to the King
KHDS	Hon. Dental Surgeon to the King
KHNS	Hon. Nursing Sister to the King
KHP	Hon. Physician to the King

KHS	Hon. Surgeon to the King; Knight, Order of the Holy Sepulchre
KM	Knight of Malta
KNH	Knight, Order of the National Hero (Antigua and Barbuda)
KNZM	Knight Companion, New Zealand Order of Merit
KP	Knight, Order of St Patrick
KPM	King's Police Medal
KStJ	Knight, Most Venerable Order of the Hospital of St John of Jerusalem
KSG	Knight, Order of St Gregory the Great
KSS	Knight, Order of St Sylvester
KT	Knight, Order of the Thistle
Kt	Knight

L

LG	Lady Companion, Order of the Garter
LitD or **LittD**	Doctor of Literature; Doctor of Letters
LLB	Bachelor of Laws
LLD	Doctor of Laws
LLM	Master of Laws
LRCP	Licentiate, Royal College of Physicians, London
LT	Lady, Order of the Thistle
LVO	Lieutenant, Royal Victorian Order

M

MA	Master of Arts
MB	Bachelor of Medicine
MBE	Member, Order of the British Empire
MBPsS	Graduate Member, British Psychological Society
MC	Military Cross
MD	Doctor of Medicine
MEC	Member of Executive Council
MEc	Master of Economics
MHA	Member of House of Assembly; Master of Health Administration
MHK	Member of the House of Keys
MHR	Member of the House of Representatives
MICE	Member, Institution of Civil Engineers
MLA	Member of Legislative Assembly; Master in Landscape Architecture

MLC	Member of Legislative Council
MM	Military Medal
MMM	Member, Order of Military Merit (Canada)
MNZM	Member, New Zealand Order of Merit
MP	Member of Parliament
MPP	Member, Provincial Parliament
MRHS	Member, Royal Horticultural Society
MRSB	Member, Royal Society of Biology
MRSC	Member, Royal Society of Chemistry
MSC	Missionaries of the Sacred Heart
MSc	Master of Science
MSM	Meritorious Service Medal; Master in Science Management
MusB or **MusBac**	Bachelor of Music
MusD	Doctor of Music
MVO	Member, Royal Victorian Order

N

NEAC	New English Art Club
NZM	New Zealand Order of Merit

O

OBC	Order of British Columbia
OBE	Officer, Order of the British Empire
OC	Officer, Order of Canada
OFM	Order of Friars Minor (Franciscans)
OFMCap	Order of Friars Minor Capuchin (Franciscans)
OFMConv	Order of Friars Minor Conventual (Franciscans)
OGS	Oratory of the Good Shepherd
OJ	Order of Jamaica
OM	Order of Merit; Order of Manitoba
OMI	Oblate of Mary Immaculate
OMM	Officer, Order of Military Merit (Canada)
ONZ	Order of New Zealand
ONZM	Officer, New Zealand Order of Merit
OOnt	Order of Ontario
OP	*Ordinis Praedicatorum* (of the Order of Preachers (Dominican))
OQ	Officer, National Order of Quebec
OSA	Order of St Augustine (Augustinian)

OSB	Order of St Benedict (Benedictine)
OSFC	Franciscan (Capuchin) Order

P

PC	Privy Counsellor
PhD	Doctor of Philosophy

Q

QC	Queen's Counsel
QFSM	Queen's Fire Service Medal for Distinguished Service
QGM	Queen's Gallantry Medal
QHC	Honorary Chaplain to the Queen
QHDS	Honorary Dental Surgeon to the Queen
QHP	Honorary Physician to the Queen
QHS	Honorary Surgeon to the Queen
QPM	Queen's Police Medal
QSM	Queen's Service Medal (NZ)
QSO	Queen's Service Order (NZ)

R

RA	Royal Academician
RAF	Royal Air Force
RAM	(Member of) Royal Academy of Music
RBA	Member, Royal Society of British Artists
RCamA	Member, Royal Cambrian Academy
RD	Royal Naval Reserve Decoration
RDI	Royal Designer for Industry (Royal Society of Arts)
RE	Fellow, Royal Society of Painter-Printmakers
RGN	Registered General Nurse
RHA	Royal Hibernian Academy; Royal Horse Artillery
RI	(Member of) Royal Institute of Painters in Water Colours
RIBA	(Member of) Royal Institute of British Architects
RICS	(Member of) Royal Institution of Chartered Surveyors
RM	Royal Marines; Registered Midwife
RMN	Registered Mental Nurse
RN	Royal Navy; Registered Nurse
RNT	Registered Nurse Tutor
ROI	Member, Royal Institute of Oil Painters
RP	(Member of) Royal Society of Portrait Painters

RRC	Royal Red Cross
RSA	Royal Scottish Academician
RSCN	Registered Sick Children's Nurse
RSW	Member, Royal Scottish Society of Painters in Water Colours
Rtd	Retired
RWS	(Member of) Royal Society of Painters in Water Colours

S

SC	Star of Courage (Canada); Senior Counsel
ScD	Doctor of Science
SCF	Senior Chaplain to the Forces
SCM	Silver Crown of Merit (Barbados); State Certified Midwife
SEN	State Enrolled Nurse
SGM	Sea Gallantry Medal
SJ	Society of Jesus (Jesuits)
SJD	Doctor of Juristic Science
SOM	Saskatchewan Order of Merit (Canada)
SOSc	Society of Ordained Scientists
SRN	State Registered Nurse
SRP	State Registered Physiotherapist
SSC	Solicitor before Supreme Court (Scotland)
SSF	Society of St Francis
SSJE	Society of St John the Evangelist
SSM	Society of the Sacred Mission
STD	*Sacrae Theologiae Doctor* (Doctor of Sacred Theology)

T

TD	Territorial Efficiency Decoration; Efficiency Decoration (T&AVR) (since April 1967); Teachta Dala (Member of the Dáil, Eire)
ThD	Doctor of Theology
TSD	Tertiary of St Dominic

U

UJD	*Utriusque Juris Doctor*, Doctor of both Laws (Doctor of Canon and Civil Law)

V

VA	Royal Order of Victoria and Albert
VC	Victoria Cross
VD	Volunteer Officers' Decoration; Victorian Decoration
VG	Vicar-General
VL	Vice Lord-Lieutenant
VRD	Royal Naval Volunteer Reserve Officers' Decoration

W

WRAC	Women's Royal Army Corps
WRAF	Women's Royal Air Force
WRNS	Women's Royal Naval Service
WS	Writer to the Signet

Y

yr	younger

ROYALTY

A writer not personally known to the Queen or other member of the Royal Family should address his letter to the Private Secretary, Equerry or Lady in Waiting of the person concerned, asking that the subject of the letter be made known to Her Majesty (or to His or Her Royal Highness).

The Queen

In speech	On presentation to the Queen the subject does not start the conversation. He or she will answer, using in the first instance the title Your Majesty, and subsequently Ma'am.
In writing	*Letter*
	Madam, *or*
	May it please Your Majesty,
	I have the honour to remain, Madam,
	Your Majesty's most humble and obedient subject,
	Envelope
Formally	(For formal or State documents only)
	To The Queen's Most Excellent Majesty
Otherwise	To Her Majesty The Queen

The Duke of Edinburgh

The Duke is entitled to the style of a Prince of the Blood Royal, as His Royal Highness The Prince Philip, Duke of Edinburgh.

In speech	The same rules apply as for the Queen, the title used in the first instance being Your Royal Highness, and subsequently Sir.
In writing	*Letter*
	Sir,
	I have the honour to remain, Sir,
	Your Royal Highness's most humble and obedient servant,

In writing   *Envelope*

To His Royal Highness The Prince Philip, Duke of
Edinburgh

Princes and Princesses of the Blood Royal, and Dukes and Duchesses of the Blood Royal

---

Princes and Dukes of the Blood Royal

Persons related by birth to a hereditary monarch are 'of the blood royal'. The sons, brothers and uncles of the sovereign are princes of the blood royal; the daughters, sisters and aunts are princesses of the blood royal.

Royal peerages (dukedoms or earldoms) are created for sons and male-line grandsons, usually upon coming of age or upon marriage. Royal peers remain princes but it is advisable to use the style employed by the Crown. Royal status is indicated by the HRH style. For example, Prince William should be addressed as HRH the Duke of Cambridge.

Prince William's wife, Catherine, is styled HRH the Duchess of Cambridge. Through marriage she is 'Princess William' because she takes her husband's rank and title, but as she is not 'of the blood royal' she is not 'Princess Catherine'.

In speech   For all royal princes the same rules apply as for the
Queen, the title used in the first instance being Your
Royal Highness, and subsequently Sir. Royal princesses,
whether married or unmarried, are called in the first
instance Your Royal Highness, and subsequently
Ma'am.

In writing   *Letter*

Sir (or Madam),

I have the honour to remain, Sir (or Madam),

Your Royal Highness's most humble and obedient
servant,

In writing   *Envelope*

To His (or Her) Royal Highness the Prince (or Princess)
. . . *or*

To His (or Her) Royal Highness the Duke (or Duchess) of
. . .

Camilla, Duchess of Cornwall

As the second wife of the Prince of Wales, she chose to use her husband's secondary designation, rather than 'Princess of Wales', and is styled HRH The Duchess of Cornwall.

In speech The same rules apply as for Duchesses (page 15).
and writing

GLOSSARY: Peerage

Abeyance: a title which is in a state of suspension between co-heirs.

Baronetage: hereditary Order of Baronets, created in 1611 by James I.

Collaterals: relations of the peer or baronet which are more remote than brothers or uncles, for example first cousins and kinsmen.

Courtesy title: the style of address used by the children of a duke, marquess or earl; they do not hold their own title but use the title through custom or courtesy.

Decoration: a medal or order awarded to honour a recipient. It might be civil, military or state.

Devolving title: a title passing down from one person to another, for example from father to son.

Dignity: a high office or rank.

Dormant: if a peer dies and heirs cannot be traced but are believed to exist, or there is insufficient evidence to prove a claim to the title is legitimate, the peerage falls dormant.

Earl Marshal: a Great Officer of State with authority over the College of Arms.

Extinct: if a peer dies and no heir with a direct descent from the first peer is eligible to inherit, the title becomes extinct and reverts to The Crown.

Garter King of Arms: the chief herald at the College of Arms, responsible for the granting of new coats of arms and maintaining a register of arms, pedigrees and genealogies for England, Wales and Northern Ireland.

Gazetted: a new title officially announced or published in the London Gazette.

Heir apparent: the eldest son, the eldest surviving son (where a deceased elder brother has left no heir) or the only son of the holder of a title.

Heir presumptive: the next in line who could be displaced in succession by the birth of an heir apparent.

Heiress presumptive: when a title may pass in the female line, a daughter is heiress presumptive until a son is born. If there is more than one daughter but no son, they are co-heirs to an English Barony, created by writ of summons.

Knightage: non-hereditary knights which can be one of the higher classes of the Orders of Chivalry or the ancient title of Knight Bachelor.

Letters Patent: a document issued by the Sovereign by which peerage titles are granted.

London Gazette: official newspaper of the United Kingdom government in which statutory notices are required to be published. It is Britain's oldest continuously published newspaper.

Lord Great Chamberlain: a Great Officer of State with authority over the Palace of Westminster.

Lord Lyon King of Arms: a Great Officer of State and the chief heraldic officer of Scotland, dealing with all matters relating to Scottish Heraldry and Coats of Arms.

Nobility: a class of persons of elevated rank holding hereditary titles.

Order of Chivalry: in medieval times, a society or fellowship of knights in imitation of the military orders of the Crusades. In modern times, orders of merit are established by monarchs or governments to bestow honours on deserving individuals; each order may have several classes.

Peerage: a peer holds one or more titles (duke, marquess, earl, viscount, baron) inherited from a direct ancestor or bestowed upon him by the monarch. The separate peerages of England and Scotland were combined as the Peerage of Great Britain in 1707; the separate peerage of Ireland combined with Great Britain in 1801 to form the Peerage of the United Kingdom.

Precedence: a list of titles which sets out the order of rank for formal occasions. It can be used when deciding the order in which guests arrive and for seating plans.

Primogeniture: the right of the eldest child, especially the eldest son, to inherit the estate of one or both parents.

Remainder: a description in the letters patent which specifies how the title may descend after the death of a peer, for example to male heirs only or to include female heirs. A Special Remainder is a clause which allows for a variation from the normal.

Spiritual peerage: the Archbishops of Canterbury and York, the Bishops of London, Durham and Winchester, and 21 of the longest-serving English diocesan bishops are ex-officio members of the House of Lords. When they retire (compulsory at 70) their membership of the House of Lords ceases.

Temporal peerage: a secular peerage as opposed to a spiritual peerage; the Lords Temporal are made up of elected hereditary peers, life peers, law lords, the Earl Marshal and the Lord Great Chamberlain.

Warrant: an order serving as legal authorisation.

THE PEERAGE: General Notes

The peerage has five descending, hereditary degrees. They are **Dukes, Marquesses, Earls, Viscounts and Barons**. We will begin with some general remarks applying to all degrees before taking the five degrees in turn. Rules for each separately appear in sections beginning on pages 15, 23, 31, 38 and 43.

Peers and the House of Lords   Since the House of Lords Act 1999, only ninety hereditary peers still sit in the House of Lords. Today the majority of peers active in the House of Lords are the **Life Peers** (page 8) and the **Lords Spiritual** (page 73). The **Law Lords** (page 130) were normally members of the legal profession on whom a peerage had been conferred but since 2009 they are disqualified from sitting or voting in the House of Lords until their retirement from the Supreme Court.

Devolving titles

A hereditary title descends only in the oldest direct line, that is from father to son, or grandfather to grandson, except in such instances as will be mentioned, in which descent also includes the female line, and those in which remainder is expressly granted.

In the case of an ancient peerage, succession sometimes devolves upon a distant cousin, but he succeeds not because he is a cousin of the preceding peer, but because he is descended from some former holder of the title.

The brother or nephew of a newly created peer would not succeed to his honours unless special remainder were granted to his Patent, nor would a cousin of an older creation, unless his descent were from a former holder of it. This explains why some peers succeeding take lower titles than their predecessors.

Courtesy titles

All peers have a family name as well as their titles, although in numerous cases, especially in the lower ranks of the peerage, the two are the same. The family name is used by the sons and daughters of peers, except in the cases of eldest sons of dukes, marquesses and earls.

In almost every case peers of these three categories have lesser titles also, of which the eldest son usually takes the highest as his courtesy title and uses it in every way as if it were his by right. In the few cases where there are no second titles, as in the earldoms of Devon,

Huntingdon, and Temple of Stowe, the family name is used as a courtesy title.

The eldest son of a duke is born in the degree of a marquess, but his courtesy title depends upon his father's lesser dignities. He takes the highest of these, which may be only that of an earl, a viscount, or a baron. He takes his title from birth, and, when he marries, his wife becomes a marchioness or a countess, or whatever it may be, and his children take the titles attached to those ranks. The eldest son of an eldest son takes a third title from the ducal collection, but of a lower grade than that of his father.

The correct ways of using these titles will be found under their various headings. They are in all respects the same, whether they are actual or courtesy titles, except that the prefixes, Most Honourable and Right Honourable, or The (which stands in their place; *see* page 10), are not used for courtesy titles.

Peer titles

Most peers hold more than one title and will use the most senior one. Lesser titles are available for their heirs to use as courtesy titles.

Examples

12th Duke of Northumberland (Ralph George Algernon Percy) has the family name Percy. He succeeded his elder brother, the 11th Duke, in 1995. He is addressed on an envelope as His Grace the Duke of Northumberland.

His ducal collection includes the lesser titles of: Earl of Northumberland, Baron Warkworth, Earl Percy, Earl of Beverley, Lord Lovaine, and Baron of Alnwick.

His eldest son and heir (George Dominic Percy) uses the courtesy title Earl Percy.

His other children are Lady Catherine Percy, Lady Melissa Percy, and Lord Max Percy.

His wife is Her Grace the Duchess of Northumberland.

8th Marquess of Exeter (William Michael Anthony Cecil) has the family name Cecil. He succeeded his father, the 7th Marquess, in 1988. He is addressed on an envelope as The Most Hon. the Marquess of Exeter.

He also holds the lesser titles of: Baron Burghley, and Earl of Exeter.

His eldest son and heir (Anthony John Cecil) uses the courtesy title Lord Burghley.

His other child is Lady Angela Cecil.

His wife is The Most Hon. the Marchioness of Exeter.

Addressing the Heir on Succession

Until after his predecessor's funeral it is customary to continue to address the heir of a peerage or baronetcy by the courtesy title or other style by which he was formerly known.

Collaterals

All courtesy titles, or titles connected with the family name of a peer, are attached only to the actual descendants of that peer, with one occasional exception. It is that when a peer is succeeded by other than a son, the new peer's brothers and sisters may take the titles that would have been theirs if their father had succeeded.* In such cases he would have succeeded had he lived, so the honour really comes through him. His widow, however, if he has left one, does not share this privilege.

For instance, the 8th Duke of Devonshire died without issue. His heir was the eldest son of his brother, Lord Edward Cavendish, who had predeceased him. As long as the 8th duke lived his heir presumptive had no title, nor of course had his two brothers. But when Mr Victor Cavendish succeeded to the dukedom, his brothers became Lord Richard and Lord John Cavendish. His mother, however, remained Lady Edward Cavendish.

*These privileges cannot be claimed as a right. They are given by favour of the Crown, and warrants are granted in such cases only upon the recommendation of the Home Secretary.

Life Peers

Life peers rank with hereditary barons and baronesses according to the date of their creation. Wives of life peers take the title of Lady, and their children The Honourable. Husbands of women life peers do not take any title. Children of women life peers, however, take the title The Honourable. In all respects, except that the title does not descend, rules as for **Barons** and **Baronesses** apply (*see* page 43).

Life Peers

Life peers were introduced under the Life Peerages Act of 1958 and it gave women the right to a seat in the House of Lords for the first time. Life peers now outnumber hereditary peers.

The House of Lords Act 1999 removed the right to an automatic seat in the House of Lords for those who had inherited it (except the Earl Marshal and the Lord Great Chamberlain so they are able to carry out their ceremonial functions), but as a compromise ninety-two hereditary peers were elected to remain. Ten hereditary peers were given life peerages, allowing them to sit in the House of Lords even though not elected.

The House of Lords Reform Act 2014 provided for members of the House of Lords to resign, retire or to be excluded. They retain their titles, however.

Title usage

It should be noted that personal preference can overrule custom and form. For example, the 13th Marquess of Lothian, who is entitled to sit as a Life Peer in the House of Lords as Baron Kerr of Monteviot, prefers to be styled as 'The Rt Hon. Michael Ancram'.

A peer might prefer a less formal mode of address for professional or modesty reasons, or to avoid overtones of privilege; others might consider their formal title infers seniority. However, the form 'Lord Alan Sugar' is incorrect and should never be used.

Territorial Additions

All peerages have still, as in their origin, a territorial basis, which is expressed in the Letters Patent creating a new peerage, as Baron Smith, of (a place with which the new Baron has connections) in the County of . . . . This, which may be described as the 'address' of the peerage, does not form part of the title, and should never be used as though it did. There is, however, an increasing tendency to do so.

Some peerages, however, have a territorial addition included in their titles, to avoid confusion with older peerages of the same name (whether or not these still survive). In these cases, of which the Baronies of Morris, Morris of Aberavon, Morris of Handsworth, and Morris of Kenwood make a good example, the Letters Patent will read, e.g. Baron Morris of Handsworth, of Handsworth in the County of West Midlands, and it will be clear that the territorial addition forms part of the title, and should be used in addressing or referring to the peer. It is not possible for peers to change their titles from the form in which they were first created.

(*See also* page 60 for the Scottish use of territorial additions.)

New Peerages

When a new peerage is created, it is not possible to address the new peer as Lord or Lady . . . immediately, because the title must be decided and the Letters Patent prepared. The new title will then be gazetted. If Hilary Smith receives a peerage, he or she retains the existing form of address until becoming, e.g. Baron(ess) Smith of Newtown; no title can be used until the actual title is known. (But *see* page 59 for new knighthoods, etc).

Disclaiming of Hereditary Peerages

The Peerage Act of 1963 authorised the disclaimer for life of certain hereditary peerages. A peer who disclaims his peerage loses all titles and precedence attached to it; he cannot, however, disclaim a baronetcy or a knighthood, and if he possesses one will be known by the appropriate title. His wife also loses the title and precedence which she received from her husband's hereditary peerage, although not, of course, any title and precedence she may herself have possessed. The eldest son of a disclaimed peer may continue if he wishes to use the courtesy title he used previously, and other children to use the titles Lord, Lady or The Honourable.

Disclaiming of hereditary peerages: Rt Hon. Tony Benn

Rt Hon. Tony Benn was the elder surviving son of 1st Viscount Stansgate. His brother had been the heir but was killed in the Second World War. When his father died in 1960 he was already a Member of the House of Commons and on succeeding to the title he automatically lost his seat. He won a by-election in May 1961 only to be prevented from taking his seat. He instigated an Act to make a disclaimer possible and disclaimed his title for life in 1963. On Tony Benn's death in 2014, his son chose to use the title 3rd Viscount Stansgate.

The Prefix 'The'

Members of the peerage are entitled by ancient custom, almost amounting to a right, to the following appellations:

> Dukes – The Most Noble . . .
>
> Marquesses – The Most Honourable . . .
>
> Other Peers – The Right Honourable . . .

The practice is not to make use of the full title of peers when referring to them, but to shorten the prefix to 'The' as 'The Duke of Norfolk'.

The use of 'The Lord' is really short for 'The Most Hon. Lord' or 'The Right Hon. Lord'. When 'Lord' is used without a prefix it is for a courtesy title.

Where any peer is entitled to the additional prefix of Right Honourable by virtue of a Privy Counsellorship (*see* page 63), the addition merges in that attaching to the existing title; but Dukes and Marquesses retain the right to both their designations in legal documents and formal circumstances. 'The Right Hon.' should not be shortened to 'The' (as above) when a peer is also a Privy Counsellor; his membership of the Privy Council entitles him to the full prefix at all times. Membership of the Privy Council being an office and not an honour, the initials PC should not be appended to any name or title (*and see* page 149).

The Title 'Lady'

This is probably the commonest of all, as it is used of all peeresses under the rank of duchess, of all daughters of the three highest ranks of the peerage, and of the wives of baronets and knights. Since 1958 it has also been used of life peers, baronesses by rank.

The prefix 'The' was once by general custom used in addressing the daughters of dukes, marquesses and earls, e.g. 'The Lady Jean Smith'. The practice existed only by courtesy, and was not recognised as correct by, for example, the College of Arms; it is no longer generally used, although it would be wrong to deprive elderly ladies of the prefix should they feel strongly about it.

Widows (including Dowagers when they so wish) or former wives use their forename before the title. (See below and entries under Peerage, Baronetage and Knights.) They do not retain their husbands' titles on re-marriage.

The Title 'Honourable'

This title is a fairly frequent one, including as it does the younger sons of earls, all the sons and daughters of viscounts and barons, and the wives of the sons, beside its use outside the ranks of the peerage. The important rule to note is that it is never used in speech. Neither is it used in letter-writing, except on the envelope. (*See also* page 127 for uses outside the peerage.)

Peeresses in Their Own Right

Some baronies and a few earldoms descend in the female line. A peeress in her own right is addressed exactly as though the rank were obtained through marriage.

Husbands and Children of Peeresses in Their Own Right

Husbands take no style or dignity from their wives. Their children, however, are addressed in all respects as if the peerage were held by their father.

Dowagers

These rules apply to the five grades of the peerage and also to the baronetage.

A dowager peeress is the earliest surviving widow of a preceding holder of the title, irrespective of her relationship to the existing holder. She may thus be mother, grandmother, aunt, great-aunt, etc.

Example   The Dowager Duchess of Middlesex

Socially, however, a dowager peeress may prefer to be known not as Dowager, but by her forename; it is necessary to find out which style she prefers but in case of doubt the use of her forename is recommended.

Where a Dowager is alive, succeeding widows use their forename.

Example   Mary, Duchess of Middlesex

If the existing peer has no wife, the widow of his predecessor usually prefers to be addressed as if her husband were still alive, without prefix or forename.

When the Dowager dies, the next senior widow becomes the Dowager.

In Scotland the style of Dowager is applied only where the peeress is mother or grandmother of the present peer; it is carefully retained in Scottish families, since it emphasises that the widow became ancestress of an heir.

In the past, a dowager peeress would have made an announcement in the press of the style of address she preferred, but this practice has fallen out of favour.

Former Wives of Peers

The wife of a peer whose marriage has been dissolved uses her forename.

Example   Mary, Duchess of Middlesex

Peeresses Re-marrying

A peeress who re-marries loses the title she acquired by marriage to a peer; but retains or resumes any title she previously bore in her own right, or as the daughter of a peer.

Husbands and Children of Peers' Daughters

A husband's name or status is not altered in any way by his wife's degree. The children have no distinctions of any sort through their mother.

Peerage of Scotland

The Peerage of Scotland (that is, peerages created in Scotland before the Act of Union of 1707) has two distinctive features.

The lowest grade of the peerage is not Baron (which in Scots law denotes the property of a territorial estate held by Baronial charter), but Lord of Parliament. This should not be confused with the judicial title given to a Judge of the Court of Session in Scotland (*see* page 134). In practice the difference has little effect, since Barons are known and addressed as Lord in any case; but where it is desired to show the exact title, it is, in the case of Scottish lordships created before 1707, not 'Baron Gray' (for example), but 'Lord Gray'. Scottish Lords and Ladies and their families are addressed in all ways the same as Barons and Baronesses (*see* page 43), with the exception which follows.

The second feature peculiar to Scottish peerages is the title of Master given to the heir, whether apparent or presumptive (also to the eldest son of an heir who bears a courtesy title). The heir to a Duke, a Marquess or an Earl who is entitled to use a courtesy title will do so, rather than be known as Master of . . . ; but the heir to a Viscount or Lord, and the eldest son of a Viscount or Lord by courtesy, is known as Master. The title is nearly always derived from that to which the bearer is heir; thus Viscount Falkland's heir is the Master of Falkland, and Lord Napier and Ettrick's the Master of Napier. Their wives are called The Hon. Mrs . . ., without the husband's forename.

Example   The Master of Ballantrae

The Hon. Mrs Scott of Ballantrae

In speech   Formerly styled 'My Lord', the Master is nowadays called Sir on formal occasions, otherwise by his surname, Mr Scott. In the household and family he is referred to as The Master. His wife is called Mrs Scott.

In writing	*Letter*
Formally	Sir (or Dear Sir), Madam,
Socially	Dear Mr Scott,
	Dear Mrs Scott,
	Envelope
	The Master of Ballantrae
	The Hon. Mrs Scott of Ballantrae

THE PEERAGE:
Dukes and Duchesses

The titles of all existing dukedoms are taken from the name of a place. (There are no instances of the title being taken from the family name. In those cases where the two are the same, the family name has been taken from the place.)

Example   To help us in our explanation we will create a Duke of Middlesex, who is also Marquess of Huddersfield and Earl of Ramsgate, to name only his principal titles. His family name shall be Smith.

The formal style of a Duke is 'The Most Noble the Duke of . . .', but the form of address for those of social equality is Duke of Middlesex or Duchess of Middlesex, the necessity for using the full title generally being avoided. For instance, if there is no need to distinguish between different dukes and duchesses, plain Duke or Duchess is correct. They are referred to as The Duke or The Duchess.

The archaic style of the title in conjunction with a forename, e.g. Duke John, is not now used. To distinguish a particular duke from others of his line he is called John, Duke of . . . , or The Second Duke of . . . .

In speech	In conversation it is best to make as sparing a use as possible of titles. Formally addressed as Your Grace, they are referred to as His Grace and Her Grace.
In writing	*Letter*
Formally	My Lord Duke,
	I remain,
	Your Grace's most obedient servant,
	Madam,
	I remain,
	Your Grace's most obedient servant,
In writing	*Letter*
Less formally	My Lord Duke,
	Yours faithfully,
	Madam,
	Yours faithfully,
Socially	Dear Duke of Middlesex,
	Yours sincerely,

or more familiarly

Dear Duke,

Yours sincerely,

Dear Duchess of Middlesex,

Yours sincerely,

or more familiarly

Dear Duchess,

Yours sincerely,

Envelope

Formally   His Grace the Duke of Middlesex

Her Grace the Duchess of Middlesex

Socially   The prefix His Grace or Her Grace may be omitted, but The should then be retained.

Dowager Duchesses

A dowager duchess is so called when she is the earliest surviving widow of a preceding duke, irrespective of her relationship to the reigning duke (*but see* page 12 for Scottish practice).

Example   The Dowager Duchess of Middlesex

Later surviving widows are distinguished by the use of their forename before the title (see page 12).

Example   Mary, Duchess of Middlesex

But if the existing duke has no wife, the widow of his predecessor is addressed in all respects as if her husband were alive.

Example   The Duchess of Middlesex

In speech   The rules for addressing in speech are in all ways the same as for the duke's wife, but if confusion were threatened she would be referred to as The Dowager Duchess.

In writing   *Letter*

Formally   Madam,

I remain,

Your Grace's most obedient servant,

	or
	Madam,
	Yours faithfully,
Socially	Dear Duchess of Middlesex,
	Yours sincerely,
	or more familiarly
	Dear Duchess,
	Yours sincerely,
	Envelope
Formally	Her Grace the Dowager Duchess of Middlesex *or*
	Her Grace Mary, Duchess of Middlesex
Socially	The prefix Her Grace may be omitted but The should then be retained.

Former Wives of Dukes

In speech	They are addressed as Madam or Duchess; referred to as Mary, Duchess of Middlesex.
In writing	*Letter*
Formally	Madam,
	I remain, Madam,
	Your most obedient servant,
	or
	Madam,
	Yours faithfully,
Socially	Dear Duchess of Middlesex,
	Yours sincerely,
	or more familiarly
	Dear Duchess,
	Yours sincerely,
	Envelope
	Mary, Duchess of Middlesex

Eldest Sons of Dukes

(*See also* under **Courtesy Titles**, page 6)

The eldest son of a duke is born in the degree of a marquess, but his courtesy title depends upon his father's lesser dignities. He normally takes the highest of these, which may be only that of an earl or lesser degree. He takes his title from birth, and, when he marries, his wife and children share the honours attached to his rank.

Example   The eldest son of our Duke of Middlesex would be Marquess of Huddersfield and his wife Marchioness of Huddersfield. Their eldest son would be Earl of Ramsgate.

The correct use of these titles will be found under their various headings. It is in all respects the same, whether they are actual or courtesy titles, except that the prefix Most Honourable, or 'The', which represents it, is not used, i.e. Marquess of Huddersfield, not The Most Honourable the Marquess of Huddersfield. (*See* page 10.)

Widows of Eldest Sons of Dukes, and Former Wives of Eldest Sons of Dukes

Rules will vary according to the title of the Eldest Son.

Children of Eldest Sons of Dukes

The eldest son takes a third title from the ducal collection, of a lower grade than that of his father. Titles of his brothers and sisters will depend on the father's title.

Daughters and Younger Sons of Dukes

The younger sons of a duke bear the title 'Lord' with their forename and family names, and all daughters of a duke bear the title 'Lady'.

Examples   Lord John Smith

Lady Barbara Smith

In this category the commonest mistakes are made by those who do not know the distinctions between the sorts of people who are entitled to be called 'Lord' or 'Lady'. Lord John Smith must never be called Lord Smith, nor Lady Barbara Smith be called Lady Smith.

In speech   When the full titles are not used they are called Lord John and Lady Barbara. There is no other abbreviation unless one is on such terms of intimacy as to use their forenames alone.

In writing	*Letter*
Formally	My Lord,
	I have the honour to remain,
	Your Lordship's obedient servant,
	My Lady (or Madam),
	I have the honour to remain,
	Your Ladyship's obedient servant,
In writing	*Letter*
Less formally	My Lord,
	Yours faithfully,
	Madam,
	Yours faithfully,
Socially	Dear Lord John Smith,
	Yours sincerely,
	or more familiarly
	Dear Lord John,
	Yours sincerely,
Socially	Dear Lady Barbara Smith,
	Yours sincerely,
	or more familiarly
	Dear Lady Barbara,
	Yours sincerely,
	Envelope
	Lord John Smith
	Lady Barbara Smith

Wives of Younger Sons of Dukes

The mistake already alluded to in this category is made most often in the case of wives of younger sons of dukes and marquesses. The wife of Lord John Smith is Lady John Smith, and never in any circumstances Lady Smith. She is known less formally as Lady John. This rule is varied only when she is of higher rank than her husband, in which case her own forename is substituted for his (*See* under **Married Daughters of Dukes**, page 21.)

In speech	Lady John Smith
	or more familiarly
	Lady John
In writing	*Letter*
Formally	Madam (or My Lady),
	I have the honour to remain,
	Your Ladyship's obedient servant,
Less formally	Madam,
	Yours faithfully,
Socially	Dear Lady John Smith,
	Yours sincerely,
	or more familiarly
	Dear Lady John
	Yours sincerely,
	Envelope
	Lady John Smith

Widows of Younger Sons of Dukes

If the widow of a younger son of a duke, having no title of her own, re-marries, she may not continue to use her late husband's name and title. If, on the other hand, she has a title of her own, she will use it coupled with her new name. If she re-marries into the peerage, she will obviously share her second husband's name and title.

Former Wives of Younger Sons of Dukes

The same rules apply to former wives as to widows.

Children of Younger Sons of Dukes

The children of younger sons of dukes have no distinctions of any sort. All the sons and daughters of Lord and Lady John Smith would be plain Mr or Miss. A popular fallacy would make them honourables, but that is quite wrong. They have, of course, some precedence in the social scale.

Married Daughters of Dukes

The daughter of a duke, in marrying a peer (not a courtesy peer), shares her husband's title and precedence.

In all other cases she retains her own title of Lady with her forename even if she marries the younger son of a duke, because by a curious anomaly all peers' daughters rank one degree higher than younger sons of the same grade. In the event of marriage with the heir of an earl or lesser peer, she is entitled, if she prefers it, to retain her own title while her husband is a courtesy lord, because she actually keeps her precedence until he succeeds to his peerage. There are instances of both usages in the peerage, and the chosen style should be ascertained in each case.

Marriage with a commoner does not alter her rank in any way (nor, incidentally, that of her husband). Our duke's daughter, Lady Barbara Smith, married to Mr Peter Green, would become Lady Barbara Green. In no circumstances would she be called Lady Peter Green. Together they would be referred to as Mr Peter and Lady Barbara Green, or Mr and Lady Barbara Green.

Curiously enough, however, the daughter of a duke (as also of a marquess or earl) keeps her rank as such in the table of precedence if she marries out of the peerage, but exchanges it for that of her husband if she remains in it, even if it means descending several steps. Thus Lady Barbara having married Mr Peter Green, would go in to dinner before a sister who had married a baron.

Examples

Marriage with:	Husband's name:	His wife's name will be:
a commoner	Peter Green, Esq.	Lady Barbara Green
Scottish chief or laird	James MacBrown of Glenbrown	Lady Barbara MacBrown of Glenbrown
a knight or baronet	Sir Bernard Brown	Lady Barbara Brown
a younger son of an earl or lesser peer	The Honourable George Wilson	Lady Barbara Wilson
an eldest son of an earl	Viscount Staines (Lord Staines)	Lady Barbara Staines, *or* Viscountess Staines (Lady Staines), as she prefers

a younger son of a duke or marquess	Lord John Bull	Lady Barbara Bull
an eldest son of a marquess	Earl of Malvern (Lord Malvern)	Countess of Malvern (Lady Malvern) or Lady Barbara Malvern, as she prefers
an eldest son of a duke	Marquess of Mere (Lord Mere)	Marchioness of Mere (Lady Mere)
a peer of any rank	The Right Hon. Lord Slough (The Lord Slough)	The Right Hon. Lady Slough (The Lady Slough)

Children of Daughters of Dukes

The children of daughters of dukes receive no titles or distinctions of any sort through their mother.

THE PEERAGE:
Marquesses and Marchionesses

This title is rendered in two ways, marquess or marquis. The former is the older and purely British. Peers of this rank use which form they prefer, and their choice should be ascertained and observed in addressing them.

Territorial/non-Territorial Titles

The title of marquess is generally taken from the name of a place, as it invariably is in the case of a duke.

Example   The Marquess of Montgomeryshire

There are two marquessates in our peerage, however, whose titles are taken from the family names, and in both these cases the preposition is dropped, thus:

The Marquess Conyngham

The Marquess Townshend

In one other case there is no preposition even though the title is territorial, viz.,

The Marquess Camden

Example   Our typical peer of this, the second grade, shall be the Marquess of Montgomeryshire, who is also the Earl of Malvern and Baron Swindon. His family name shall be Evans.

In speech   It has been said already that all peers and peeresses below ducal rank are called Lord and Lady in speech. This brings us to a mistake quite commonly made in connection with the lower grades of the peerage. Although it is correct to talk of the Duke, or Duchess of Middlesex – indeed, they could not be referred to in any other way – the rule is quite different for the marquessate. The Marquess and Marchioness of Montgomeryshire would always be addressed as My Lord and My Lady, and referred to as Lord and Lady Montgomeryshire. There are a few formal occasions on which the full title would be used, but it would never occur socially.

In writing	*Letter*
Formally	My Lord Marquess, *or*
	My Lord,
	I have the honour to remain,
	Your Lordship's obedient servant,
	Madam,
	I have the honour to remain,
	Your Ladyship's obedient servant,
Less formally	My Lord,
	Yours faithfully,
	Madam,
	Yours faithfully,
Socially	Dear Lord Montgomeryshire, *or*
	Dear Montgomeryshire,
	Yours sincerely,
	Dear Lady Montgomeryshire,
	Yours sincerely,
	Envelope
Formally	The Most Hon. the Marquess of Montgomeryshire
	The Most Hon. the Marchioness of Montgomeryshire
Socially	The Marquess of Montgomeryshire
	The Marchioness of Montgomeryshire

Dowager Marchionesses

A dowager marchioness is so called when she is the earliest surviving widow of a preceding marquess, irrespective of her relationship to the present marquess (*but see* page 12 for Scottish practice). A later surviving widow is distinguished by the use of her forename before her title (*see* page 12).

Examples	The Dowager Marchioness of Montgomeryshire
	Enid, Marchioness of Montgomeryshire
In speech	Both would be addressed as Madam and referred to as Lady Montgomeryshire.

In writing	*Letter*
Formally	Madam,
	I have the honour to remain,
	Your Ladyship's obedient servant,
Less formally	Madam,
	Yours faithfully,
Socially	Dear Lady Montgomeryshire,
	Yours sincerely,
	Envelope
Formally	The Most Hon. the Dowager Marchioness of Montgomeryshire *or*
	The Most Hon. Enid, Marchioness of Montgomeryshire
Socially	The Dowager Marchioness of Montgomeryshire *or*
	Enid, Marchioness of Montgomeryshire

Former Wives of Marquesses

The former wife of a Marquess uses her forename before the title unless she re-marries.

In speech	She is addressed as Madam and referred to as Lady Montgomeryshire.
In writing	*Letter*
Formally	Madam,
	I have the honour to remain,
	Your Ladyship's obedient servant,
Less formally	Madam,
	Yours faithfully,
Socially	Dear Lady Montgomeryshire,
	Yours sincerely,
	Envelope
Formally	Enid, Marchioness of Montgomeryshire
Socially	Enid, Marchioness of Montgomeryshire

Eldest Sons of Marquesses

(*See also* under **Courtesy Titles**, page 6)

As stated elsewhere, peers in this category have lesser titles as well, and the eldest son usually takes the highest of these as his courtesy title, which is used in every way as if it were his by right. He takes the title from birth, and on his marriage his wife and children share the honours attached to his rank. His eldest son would take a third title from among the marquess's lesser titles.

Example　The eldest son of our Marquess of Montgomeryshire would be Earl of Malvern and his wife Countess of Malvern. Their eldest son would be Baron Swindon. The correct use of these titles will be found under their various headings. It is in all respects the same, whether they are actual or courtesy titles, except that the prefix Right Honourable, or 'The', which represents it, is not used, e.g. Earl of Malvern (*see* page 10).

Widows of Eldest Sons of Marquesses, Former Wives of Eldest Sons of Marquesses, and Children of Eldest Sons of Marquesses

Rules will vary according to the title of the Eldest Son.

Younger Sons of Marquesses

The younger sons of a marquess bear the title Lord and their forename and family name.

Example　Lord Charles Evans

Lord Charles Evans must never be called Lord Evans.

In speech	When the full title is not used, he is called Lord Charles. There is no other abbreviation.
In writing	*Letter*
Formally	My Lord,
	I have the honour to remain,
	Your Lordship's obedient servant,
Less formally	My Lord,
	Yours faithfully,
Socially	Dear Lord Charles Evans,
	Yours sincerely,

or more familiarly

Dear Lord Charles,

Yours sincerely,

Envelope

Lord Charles Evans

Wives of Younger Sons of Marquesses

The wife of Lord Charles Evans is Lady Charles Evans, and never in any circumstances Lady Evans. This rule is varied only when she is of higher rank than her husband, in which case her own forename is substituted for his. (*See under* **Married Daughters of Marquesses**, page 28.)

In speech	She is known less formally as Lady Charles.
In writing	*Letter*
Formally	Madam (or My Lady),
	I have the honour to remain,
	Your Ladyship's obedient servant,
Less formally	Madam,
	Yours faithfully,
Socially	Dear Lady Charles Evans,
	Yours sincerely,
	or more familiarly
	Dear Lady Charles,
	Yours sincerely,
	Envelope
	Lady Charles Evans

Widows and Former Wives of Younger Sons of Marquesses

If the widow of a younger son of a marquess, having no title of her own, re-marries, she may not continue to use her late husband's name and title. If, on the other hand, she has a title of her own, she will use it coupled with her new name. The same rules apply to former wives as to widows.

Children of Younger Sons of Marquesses

The children of younger sons of marquesses have no distinctions of any sort. All the sons and daughters of Lord and Lady Charles Evans would be plain Mr and Miss. They have, of course, some precedence in the social scale.

Daughters of Marquesses

All daughters of a marquess bear the title Lady with their forename and family name.

Example   Lady Joan Evans

Lady Joan Evans must never be called Lady Evans.

In speech	When the full title is not used, she is called Lady Joan. There is no other abbreviation.
In writing	*Letter*
Formally	Madam (or My Lady),
	I have the honour to remain,
	Your Ladyship's obedient servant,
Less formally	Madam,
	Yours faithfully,
Socially	Dear Lady Joan Evans,
	Yours sincerely,
	or more familiarly
	Dear Lady Joan,
	Yours sincerely,
	Envelope
	Lady Joan Evans

Married Daughters of Marquesses

The daughter of a marquess, in marrying a peer (not a courtesy peer), shares her husband's title and precedence, as also if she marries a man of equal or higher rank than her own – the eldest son of a marquess or any son of a duke. In all other cases she retains her own title of Lady with her forename, even if she marries the younger son of a marquess, because, as stated elsewhere, all peers' daughters rank one degree higher than younger sons of the same grade. In the event of marriage with the heir of an earl or lesser peer, she is entitled, if she prefers it, to retain her own title while her husband is a courtesy lord, because she actually keeps her precedence until he succeeds to his peerage. There are instances of both usages in the peerage, and the chosen style should be ascertained in each case.

Marriage with a commoner does not alter her rank in any way (nor, incidentally, that of her husband). Our marquess's daughter, married to Mr Peter Green, would become Lady Joan Green. In no circumstances would she be called Lady Peter Green. Together they would be described as Mr Peter and Lady Joan Green.

Curiously enough, however, the daughter of a marquess (as also of a duke or earl) keeps her rank as such in the table of precedence if she marries out of the peerage, but exchanges it for that of her husband if she remains in it, even if it means descending several steps. Thus Lady Joan, having married Mr Peter Green, would go in to dinner before a sister who had married a baron.

Examples

Marriage with:	*Husband's name:*	*His wife's name will be:*
a commoner	Peter Green, Esq.	Lady Joan Green
a knight or baronet	Sir Bernard Brown	Lady Joan Brown
a younger son of an earl or lesser peer	The Honourable George Wilson	Lady Joan Wilson
an eldest son of an earl	Viscount Staines (Lord Staines)	Lady Joan Staines, *or* Viscountess Staines (Lady Staines), as she prefers
a younger son of a marquess	Lord John Bull	Lady Joan Bull
an younger son of a duke	Lord John Smith	Lady John Smith, or Lady Joan Smith, as she prefers
an eldest son of a marquess	Earl of Malvern (Lord Malvern)	Countess of Malvern (Lady Malvern)
an eldest son of a duke	Marquess of Mere (Lord Mere)	Marchioness of Mere (Lady Mere)
a peer of any rank	The Right Hon. Lord Slough (The Lord Slough)	The Right Hon. Lady Slough (The Lady Slough)

Children of Daughters of Marquesses

The children of daughters of marquesses receive no titles or distinctions of any sort through their mother.

THE PEERAGE:
Earls and Countesses

This grade is sometimes territorial, sometimes taken from the family name. In the former case the preposition 'of' is generally used, and in the latter case it is not, although there are numerous exceptions to both rules.

In one or two instances, such as the Earl of Winchilsea and Nottingham, two separate earldoms have become merged. Both titles are used on all formal occasions and even on the social envelope. But in social speech and letters only the first one is employed.

The Earl of Winchilsea and Nottingham's title provides an instance of the little traps which are sometimes, almost perversely it would seem, set for the unwary. The name of the ancient town from which Lord Winchilsea takes his title is spelt Winchelsea.

Example   Our typical peer in this, the third grade, shall be the Earl of Whitby, with a second title, Viscount Staines, and the family name of Collins.

In speech	It has been remarked already that all peers and peeresses below ducal rank are called Lord and Lady in speech. This rule applies, of course, to earls and countesses, who are always referred and spoken to as Lord and Lady. As in the case of the marquessate, there are a few formal occasions on which the full title would be used, but it would never happen socially.
In writing	*Letter*
Formally	My Lord,
	I have the honour to remain,
	Your Lordship's obedient servant,
	Madam,
	I have the honour to remain,
	Your Ladyship's obedient servant,
Less formally	My Lord,
	Yours faithfully,
	Madam,
	Yours faithfully,

Socially	Dear Lord Whitby, *or*
	Dear Whitby,
	Yours sincerely,
	Dear Lady Whitby,
	Yours sincerely,
	Envelope
Formally	The Right Hon. the Earl of Whitby
	The Right Hon. the Countess of Whitby
Socially	The Earl of Whitby
	The Countess of Whitby

Dowager Countesses

A dowager countess is so called when she is the earliest surviving widow of a preceding earl (but see page 12 for Scottish practice). A later surviving widow is distinguished by the use of the forename before her title (*see* page 12).

Examples	The Dowager Countess of Whitby
	Muriel, Countess of Whitby
In speech	Style is exactly the same as if she were the present countess.
In writing	*Letter*
Formally	Madam,
	I have the honour to remain,
	Your Ladyship's obedient servant,
Less formally	Madam,
	Yours faithfully,
Socially	Dear Lady Whitby,
	Yours sincerely,
	Envelope
Formally	The Right Hon. the Dowager Countess of Whitby *or*
	The Right Hon. Muriel, Countess of Whitby
Socially	The Dowager Countess of Whitby *or*
	Muriel, Countess of Whitby

Former Wives of Earls

The former wife of an Earl uses her forename before the title.

In writing	*Letter*
Formally	Madam,
	I have the honour to remain,
	Your Ladyship's obedient servant,
Less formally	Madam,
	Yours faithfully,
Socially	Dear Lady Whitby,
	Yours sincerely,
	Envelope
	Muriel, Countess of Whitby

Eldest Sons of Earls

(*See also* under **Courtesy Titles**, page 6).

As stated elsewhere, peers in this category have lesser titles as well, and the eldest son usually takes the highest of these as his courtesy title, which is used in every way as if it were his by right. He takes the title from birth, and on his marriage his wife and children share the honours attached to his rank.

Example   The eldest son of our Earl of Whitby would be Viscount Staines and his wife Viscountess Staines. The correct use of these titles will be found under their various headings. It is in all respects the same whether they are actual or courtesy titles, with the exception that the prefix Right Honourable, or 'The', which represents it, is not used, e.g. Viscount Staines. (*See* page 10.)

Widows of Eldest Sons of Earls, Former Wives of Eldest Sons of Earls, and Children of Eldest Sons of Earls

Rules will vary according to the title of the Eldest Son.

Younger Sons of Earls

Unlike the higher grades of the peerage, younger sons of earls are styled Honourable with their forenames and family names (not initials), and there is nothing to distinguish them from the sons of viscounts and barons.

Example   The Honourable Thomas Collins

This title is never used in speech or letter-writing, except on the envelope.

The younger sons of earls are called Mr, always in conjunction with the forename.

Example   Mr Thomas Collins

In speech	The title is never used in speech, so that without inner knowledge it is difficult to recognise the rank. When it is desired to indicate it, however, a reference to the holder's parentage would be permissible.
In writing	*Letter*
Formally	Sir,
	I have the honour to remain,
	Your obedient servant,
Less formally	Dear Sir,
	Yours faithfully,
Socially	Dear Mr Collins,
	Yours sincerely,
	Envelope
	The Hon. Thomas Collins

Wives of Younger Sons of Earls

Wives of younger sons of earls share their husbands' title.

Example   The Hon. Mrs Thomas Collins

It should be carefully noted that whereas it is wrong to use the designations Mr or Miss with this title, it is right to use the designation Mrs with it.

In speech	The title is never used in speech, and the wife of Mr Thomas Collins is always alluded to as Mrs Thomas Collins. If she happens to be of higher rank than her husband, she would use her own title in conjunction with her husband's name – without the Honourable.

In writing	*Letter*
Formally	Madam,
	I have the honour to remain,
	Your obedient servant,
Less formally	Dear Madam,
	Yours faithfully,
Socially	Dear Mrs Collins,
	Yours sincerely,
	Envelope
	The Hon. Mrs Thomas Collins

Widows of Younger Sons of Earls

Widows of younger sons of earls keep their title until re-marriage, when it is abandoned in favour of the second husband's status, whether it be higher or lower. If the widow possesses a title in her own right she will of course continue to use it.

Former Wives of Younger Sons of Earls

The same rules apply to former wives as to widows.

Children of Younger Sons of Earls

Children of younger sons of earls have no distinction of any sort. They have, of course, a certain social precedence.

Daughters of Earls

Daughters of earls bear the title Lady with their forename and family names.

Example   Lady Violet Collins

In speech   The same rules apply as in the case of daughters of dukes and marquesses, viz. when the full title is not used, our earl's daughter will be called Lady Violet. There is no other abbreviation unless one is on such terms of intimacy as to use the forename alone.

In writing	*Letter*
Formally	Madam (or My Lady),
	I have the honour to remain,
	Your Ladyship's obedient servant,
Less formally	Madam,
	Yours faithfully,
Socially	Dear Lady Violet Collins,
	Yours sincerely,
	or more familiarly
	Dear Lady Violet,
	Yours sincerely,
	Envelope
	Lady Violet Collins

Married Daughters of Earls

The daughter of an earl, if she marries a peer (not a courtesy peer), or a man of equal or higher rank than her own, shares her husband's title and precedence. Otherwise she retains her own title of Lady and her forename, even if she marries the younger son of an earl, because, as stated elsewhere, all peers' daughters rank one degree higher than younger sons of the same grade. In the event of marriage with the heir of a viscount or lesser peer, she is entitled, if she prefers it, to retain her own title until her husband succeeds to his peerage, because she actually keeps her own precedence until then. In such a case the chosen style should be ascertained.

Marriage with a commoner does not alter her rank in any way (nor, incidentally, that of her husband). Our earl's daughter, married to Mr Peter Green, would become Lady Violet Green. She must never be called Lady Peter Green. Together they would be described as Mr Peter and Lady Violet Green.

Curiously enough, however, the daughter of an earl keeps her rank as such in the table of precedence if she marries out of the peerage, but exchanges it for that of her husband if she remains in it, even if it means descending several steps. Thus Lady Violet, having married Mr Peter Green, would go in to dinner before a sister who had married a baron.

Examples

Marriage with:	Husband's name:	His wife's name will be:
a commoner	Peter Green, Esq.	Lady Violet Green
a knight or baronet	Sir Bernard Brown	Lady Violet Brown
a younger son of an earl or lesser peer	The Honourable Michael O'Mara	Lady Violet O'Mara
an eldest son of an earl	Viscount Staines (Lord Staines)	Viscountess Staines (Lady Staines)
a younger son of a marquess	Lord John Bull	Lady John Bull
an younger son of a duke	Lord John Smith	Lady John Smith
an eldest son of a marquess	Earl of Malvern (Lord Malvern)	Countess of Malvern (Lady Malvern)
an eldest son of a duke	Marquess of Mere (Lord Mere)	Marchioness of Mere (Lady Mere)
a peer of any rank	The Right Hon. Lord Slough (The Lord Slough)	The Right Hon. Lady Slough (The Lady Slough)

Children of Daughters of Earls

The children of daughters of earls receive no titles or distinctions of any sort through their mother.

THE PEERAGE:
Viscounts and Viscountesses

This title is sometimes territorial, sometimes derived from the family name, but in neither case is the preposition 'of' used between the style and the title, e.g. Viscount Hereford, not The Viscount of Hereford. Viscounts in the peerage of Scotland (or before 1707) *do* include the 'of', e.g. The Viscount of Arbuthnott.

Example   Our example in this, the fourth grade of the peerage, shall be Viscount O'Mara, with the same family name.

In speech	The rule already explained, that all peers and peeresses below ducal rank are called Lord and Lady in speech, applies equally, of course, to viscounts and their wives. As in other ranks, there are a few formal occasions on which the full title would be used, but it would never happen in intimate speech.
In writing	*Letter*
Formally	My Lord,
	I have the honour to remain,
	Your Lordship's obedient servant,
	Madam,
	I have the honour to remain,
	Your Ladyship's obedient servant,
Less formally	My Lord,
	Yours faithfully,
	Madam,
	Yours faithfully,
In writing	*Letter*
Socially	Dear Lord O'Mara, *or*
	Dear O'Mara,
	Yours sincerely,
	Dear Lady O'Mara,
	Yours sincerely,

	Envelope
Formally	The Right Hon. the Viscount O'Mara
	The Right Hon. the Viscountess O'Mara
Socially	The Viscount O'Mara
	The Viscountess O'Mara

Dowager Viscountesses

A dowager viscountess is the earliest surviving widow of a preceding peer (*but see* page 12 for the Scottish practice). Later surviving widows are distinguished by the use of the forename before the title (*see* page 12).

In speech	Style is exactly the same as if she were the present viscountess (*see above*).

In writing	*Letter*
Formally	Madam,
	I have the honour to remain,
	Your Ladyship's obedient servant,
Less formally	Madam,
	Yours faithfully,
Socially	Dear Lady O'Mara,
	Yours sincerely,
	Envelope
Formally	The Right Hon. the Dowager Viscountess O'Mara *or*
	The Right Hon. Anne, Viscountess O'Mara
Socially	The Dowager Viscountess O'Mara *or*
	Anne, Viscountess O'Mara

Former Wives of Viscounts

The former wife of a Viscount uses her forename before the title.

In speech	She will be addressed as My Lady.

In writing	*Letter*
Formally	Madam,
	I have the honour to remain,
	Your Ladyship's obedient servant,

Less formally	Madam,
	Yours faithfully,
Socially	Dear Lady O'Mara,
	Yours sincerely,
	Envelope
	Anne, Viscountess O'Mara

Eldest Sons of Viscounts

Courtesy titles cease at the grade of an earl, so that the eldest son of a viscount does not take his father's second title, even if he happens to have one. Like his younger brothers, he is merely The Honourable, using his forename (not initials) and surname, and his wife shares the title.

Example	The Hon. Michael O'Mara
	The Hon. Mrs Michael O'Mara
In speech	As explained before, the title Honourable is never used in speech, so that the eldest son of our viscount would be spoken and referred to as Mr O'Mara and his wife as Mrs O'Mara.
In writing	*Letter*
Formally	Sir,
	I have the honour to remain,
	Your obedient servant,
	Madam,
	I have the honour to remain,
	Your obedient servant,
Less formally	Dear Sir,
	Yours faithfully,
	Dear Madam,
	Yours faithfully,
Socially	Dear Mr O'Mara,
	Yours sincerely,
	Dear Mrs O'Mara,
	Yours sincerely,

Envelope

The Hon. Michael O'Mara

The Hon. Mrs Michael O'Mara

Widows of Eldest Sons of Viscounts

Widows of eldest sons of viscounts keep their title until re-marriage, when it is abandoned in favour of the second husband's status, whether it be higher or lower. This does not apply, of course, if the widow possesses a title in her own right.

Former Wives of Eldest Sons of Viscounts

The same rules as above apply to former wives as to widows.

Children of Eldest Sons of Viscounts

Children of eldest sons of viscounts have no titles or distinctions of any sort. (*See* **Peerage of Scotland**, page 13).

Younger Sons of Viscounts, Wives of Younger Sons of Viscounts, Widows of Younger Sons of Viscounts, and Former Wives of Younger Sons of Viscounts

Exactly the same rules apply here as to younger sons of earls and their wives (*see* pages 33 and 34).

Children of Younger Sons of Viscounts

Children of younger sons of viscounts have no titles or distinctions of any sort.

Daughters of Viscounts

Daughters of viscounts all bear the title Honourable, like their brothers.

In speech   The title is never used in speech. The eldest daughter is referred to as Miss O'Mara, the younger ones as, e.g. Miss Nora and Miss Bridget O'Mara.

In writing   *Letter*

Style is the same for all.

Formally	Madam,
	I have the honour to remain,
	Your obedient servant,
Less formally	Dear Madam,
	Yours faithfully,
Socially	Dear Miss O'Mara,
	Yours sincerely,
In writing	*Envelope*
	The Hon. Eileen O'Mara

Married Daughters of Viscounts

The daughter of a viscount, in marrying a man of lower rank than her own, keeps her title, thus:

Marriage with:	Husband's name:	His wife's name will be:
a commoner	Mr Peter Green	The Hon. Mrs Green (not The Hon. Mrs Peter Green)
a knight or baronet	Sir Bernard Brown	The Hon. Lady Brown

In marrying a man of equal or higher rank she shares her husband's title.

Children of Daughters of Viscounts

Children of daughters of viscounts have no titles or distinctions of any sort. They have, of course, a certain social precedence.

THE PEERAGE:
Barons and Baronesses

This is the fifth and last grade of the peerage. In England and Wales 'Baron' and 'Baroness' have always been the legal terms, whereas in Scotland the legal term for a hereditary peer of this rank whose title was created before 1707 is 'Lord' or 'Lady' (*see* **Peerage of Scotland**, page 13). In usage, however, all of this rank are known as 'Lord' or 'Lady', with the exception of peeresses in their own right (including women life peers) who may choose to be called 'Baroness'.

The title is sometimes territorial, sometimes taken from the family name, and sometimes from other sources entirely.

Example   Our example shall be Baron Westley, family name Whitworth.

In speech	The rule of addressing all peers below ducal rank as Lord and Lady is equally applicable to barons and their wives. Baronesses in their own right, however (including women life peers), are called The Baroness . . . if they so wish.
In writing	*Letter*
Formally	My Lord,
	I have the honour to be,
	Your Lordship's obedient servant,
	Madam,
	I have the honour to be,
	Your Ladyship's obedient servant,
Less formally	My Lord,
	Yours faithfully,
	Madam,
	Yours faithfully,
In writing	*Letter*
Socially	Dear Lord Westley, *or*
	Dear Westley,
	Yours sincerely,

	Dear Lady Westley,
	Yours sincerely,
	Envelope
Formally	The Right Hon. Lord Westley
	The Right Hon. Lady Westley
Socially	The Lord Westley
	The Lady Westley

Dowager Baronesses

A dowager baroness is the earliest surviving widow of a preceding peer (*but see* page 12 for the Scottish practice). Later surviving widows are distinguished by the use of the forename before the title (*see* page 12).

In speech	Style is exactly the same as if she were the present baroness (see above).
In writing	*Letter*
Formally	Madam,
	I have the honour to remain,
	Your Ladyship's obedient servant,
Less formally	Madam,
	Yours faithfully,
Socially	Dear Lady Westley,
	Yours sincerely,
	Envelope
Formally	The Right Hon. the Dowager Lady Westley *or*
	The Right Hon. Anne, Lady Westley
Socially	The Dowager Lady Westley, *or*
	Anne, Lady Westley

Former Wives of Barons

The former wife of a baron uses her forename before the title.

| **In speech** | She will be addressed as My Lady. |

In writing	*Letter*
Formally	Madam,
	I have the honour to remain,
	Your Ladyship's obedient servant,
Less formally	Madam,
	Yours faithfully,
Socially	Dear Lady Westley,
	Yours sincerely,
	Envelope
	Anne, Lady Westley

Eldest Sons of Barons

Courtesy titles cease at the grade of an earl, so that the eldest son of a baron, like his younger brothers, is merely The Honourable, and his wife shares the title. 'The Honourable' is followed by a forename rather than initials.

Example	The Hon. Roger Whitworth
	The Hon. Mrs Roger Whitworth
In speech	As explained elsewhere, the title Honourable is never used in speech, so that the eldest son of our baron would be spoken and referred to as 'Mr Whitworth' and his wife as 'Mrs Whitworth'.

In writing	*Letter*
Formally	Sir,
	I have the honour to remain,
	Your obedient servant,
	Madam,
	I have the honour to remain,
	Your obedient servant,
Less formally	Dear Sir,
	Yours faithfully,
	Dear Madam,
	Yours faithfully,

Socially	Dear Mr Whitworth,
	Yours sincerely
	Dear Mrs Whitworth,
	Yours sincerely,
	Envelope
	The Hon. Roger Whitworth
	The Hon. Mrs Roger Whitworth

Widows of Eldest Sons of Barons, and Former Wives of Eldest Sons

Widows and former wives of eldest sons of barons keep their title until re-marriage, when it is abandoned in favour of the second husband's status, whether it be higher or lower. This does not apply, of course, if the widow or former wife possesses a title in her own right.

Children of Eldest Sons of Barons

Children of eldest sons of barons have no titles or distinctions of any sort. (*See* **Peerage of Scotland**, page 13.)

Younger Sons of Barons, Wives of Younger Sons of Barons, Widows of Younger Sons of Barons, and Former Wives of Younger Sons of Barons

Exactly the same rules apply here as to younger sons of earls and their wives (*see* pages 33 and 34).

Children of Younger Sons of Barons

Children of younger sons of barons have no titles or distinctions of any sort.

Daughters of Barons

All bear the title of Honourable, and the same rules apply as for daughters of viscounts (*see* page 41).

Married Daughters of Barons

The daughter of a baron, in marrying a man of lower rank than her own, keeps her title, thus:

Marriage with:	Husband's name:	His wife's name will be:
a commoner	Mr Peter Green	The Hon. Mrs Green (not The Hon. Mrs Peter Green)
a knight or baronet	Sir Bernard Brown	The Hon. Lady Brown

In marrying a man of equal or higher rank she shares her husband's title.

Children of Daughters of Barons

Children of daughters of barons have no titles or distinctions of any sort.

THE BARONETAGE

The title of baronet, identified by the prefix Sir to forename and surname, is a hereditary honour descending from father to son. If there is no son to the first holder, the title becomes extinct; but if there is no son to a later holder, the title goes to the nearest male descendant of a former holder. The title is distinguished from that of knight by the word baronet, or one of its contractions, being added at the end of the name.

Example   Sir George Robinson, Bt

Where a Scottish family uses a territorial title this is inserted before the addition 'Bt'.

Example   Sir George Robinson of Glenrobinson, Bt

The word baronet is used in full only in formal documents. Bt is the older abbreviation and the only one recognised by the Council of the Baronetage, but, in spite of this, Bart is still much used. This is a pity, because it is considered wrong by those who know and prefer the right way.

A baronet's wife takes the title of Lady in conjunction with the surname only – never with her own or her husband's forename unless she happens to have a title of her own (*see* pages 11, 21, 28, 36, 42 and 47).

Example   Lady Robinson

The only exception to this rule might be the written one of Lady (George) Robinson, when it is necessary to distinguish her from another Lady Robinson. In actual speech there can be no such distinction. In Scotland, however, the territorial addition (if it exists) acts as the distinction.

Example   Lady Robinson of Glenrobinson.

Lady Robinson is not entitled to be called The Lady Robinson (*see* page 11).

In speech   A baronet is addressed by his title and forename, as, for instance, Sir George, and spoken of as Sir George Robinson, or, more familiarly, as Sir George. There is no distinction here between a baronet and a knight.

In writing   *Letter*

Formally   Sir,

I have the honour to remain,

Your obedient servant,

	Madam,
	I have the honour to remain,
	Your Ladyship's obedient servant,
Less formally	Dear Sir,
	Yours faithfully,
	Dear Madam,
	Yours faithfully,
Socially	Dear Sir George Robinson,
	Yours faithfully,
	or more familiarly
	Dear Sir George,
	Yours sincerely,
	Dear Lady Robinson,
	Yours sincerely,
	Envelope
Formally	Sir George Robinson, Bt
	Sir George Robinson of Glenrobinson, Bt
	Lady Robinson
	Lady Robinson of Glenrobinson
Socially	Sir George Robinson, Bt
	Lady Robinson

The Baronetage

The hereditary order of baronets in England was instituted by King James I in 1611 when he offered baronetcies to gentlemen of good birth with an income of at least £1000 a year in order to raise money to pay for soldiers to carry out the pacification of Ireland. After the union of England and Scotland in 1707 new creations were styled Baronets of Great Britain; after the union of Great Britain and Ireland in 1801 new creations were styled Baronets of the United Kingdom.

The creation of baronetcies lapsed in 1964 but in 1990 the honour was given to Denis Thatcher as the husband of a Prime Minister.

The Official Roll of the Baronetage is an official list of baronets compiled by the Crown Office and published by the Standing Council of the Baronetage.

Baronetesses

There are very few baronetcies (all of them are Scottish) where it is possible for a lady to inherit the title. She is addressed in the same way as a baronet's wife, but note the following.

In writing   *Envelope*

Where for a baronet the abbreviation Bt would be added, her name should be followed by Btss.

Example   Lady Robinson of Glenrobinson, Btss

Husbands should be addressed according to their own rank or title.

Widows of Baronets

Widows of baronets retain their style of address unless and until the succeeding baronet marries, when the widow is called either

The Dowager Lady Robinson or

Dora, Lady Robinson

The rule follows that of the peerage (*see* page 12).

In speech   Style is the same as for a baronet's wife (*see* page 50).

In writing   *Letter*

Formally   Madam,

I have the honour to remain,

Your Ladyship's obedient servant,

Less formally   Dear Madam,

Yours faithfully,

Socially   Dear Lady Robinson,

Yours sincerely,

Envelope

The Dowager Lady Robinson *or*

Dora, Lady Robinson

Widows of Baronets Re-marrying

If marrying a peer, an honourable, or another baronet, the title and name of a new husband is taken. If she marries an untitled gentleman, she becomes Mrs . . . .

Former Wives of Baronets

Until re-marriage they are addressed in the same way as widows, except that they will not be Dowager, but will use a forename before the title.

Children of Baronets

Children of baronets have no titles or distinctions, except that the eldest son's forename is not used.

Example   Mr Robinson

In Scottish families which have a territorial designation (*see* page 62), he is styled 'younger' (which may be abbreviated yr) of the family description.

Example   Mr Robinson, younger of Glenrobinson

Honourables

When the son of a viscount or baron, or the younger son of an earl, receives a baronetcy, the foregoing rules apply, except as to the address of envelopes, which should be:

The Hon. Sir George Robinson, Bt

The Hon. Lady Robinson

KNIGHTS AND DAMES

The first rule for all knights or dames who have no other title is that they are addressed as Sir or Lady, with one forename and surname (Sir/Lady Evelyn Brown). The wives of knights are addressed as Lady, with the surname alone (Lady Brown). The husbands of dames are addressed according to their own title or rank.

The orders of knighthood are various, but not one of them is hereditary. We will take them in the order of their precedence and deal with general rules as they arise.

The Orders of Knighthood, in order of precedence:

The Most Noble Order of the Garter: founded in 1348 by Edward III. The origins of its name are obscure. It is limited to 25 knights.

The Most Ancient and Noble Order of the Thistle: established in 1687 by James II. It is limited to 16 knights; all must be Scottish. Women were admitted in 1987.

The Most Illustrious Order of St Patrick: created in 1783 by George III to reward those in high office in Ireland and Irish peers who supported the government. It was distinguished by the letters KP after the name and title. The Order went into abeyance with the establishment of the Irish Free State in 1922 and lapsed in 1974 with the death of the last surviving recipient.

The Most Honourable Order of the Bath: created in 1725, taking its name from the ceremonial bathing that preceded investiture in medieval times. It is awarded to state servants, with a military division and a civil division. Women were admitted in 1971.

The Most Exalted Order of the Star of India: founded in 1861 by Queen Victoria to honour Indian Princes and Chiefs, and British officers and administrators serving in India. It had three classes: Knight Grand Commander (GCSI), Knight Commander (KCSI) and Companion (CSI). No appointments have been made since 1948, and the order became dormant in 2009 with the death of the last surviving member.

The Most Distinguished Order of St Michael and St George: created in 1818 by the Prince Regent to reward service in Malta and the Ionian islands. It now includes any members of the diplomatic service and those who serve UK interests overseas.

The Most Eminent Order of the Indian Empire: founded in 1878 by Queen Victoria to reward British and Indian officials serving in India. It had three classes: Knight Grand Commander (GCIE), Knight Commander (KCIE) and Companion (CIE). No appointments have been made since 1947, after the partition of India, and the order became dormant in 2010 with the death of the last surviving member.

The Royal Victorian Order: created in 1896 by Queen Victoria and given for services to The Queen and others members of the Royal Family.

The Most Excellent Order of the British Empire: created in 1917 by George V to recognise service to the country during the First World War. It now recognises service and achievement in all fields, with a military division and a civil division.

The Most Noble Order of the Garter

This order is conferred on men and women who have contributed to the service of the United Kingdom or Commonwealth and for service to the Queen. It is distinguished by the letters KG or LG after the name and title.

Example   The Duke of Middlesex, KG

Lady Susan Braithwaite, LG

The Most Ancient and Most Noble Order of the Thistle

This order is conferred on men and women who have contributed to the Scottish nation and is distinguished by the letters KT or LT after the name and title.

Example   The Earl of Queensferry, KT

Sir William MacHector of Drimmore, KT

Lady Margaret Sutherland, LT

The Most Honourable Order of the Bath

This is the first of the orders of knighthood in which there is more than one class. Women as well as men are eligible. Members of the first two classes only are knights or dames, and the use of the title in speech and writing is the same as for baronets and their wives and children (except, of course, for the abbreviation Bt). Husbands of ladies raised to any one of the ranks in this order do not share their wives' distinctions.

MEN   **Knights**

Knights Grand Cross   Sir Robert Johnson, GCB

Knights Commanders   Sir Edward Thompson, KCB

Companions   Richard Jackson, Esq., CB

The wives of companions, as such, have no distinctions, though they have recognised precedence.

WOMEN   **Dames**

Dames Grand Cross   Dame Matilda Johnson, GCB

Dames Commanders   Dame Pamela Thompson, DCB

Companions   Mrs Jackson, CB

The title carried by the first two degrees of this order is used always in conjunction with the lady's forename.

In speech   The formal mode of address is 'Dame Matilda' or 'Dame Pamela'.

In writing   *Letter*

Formally   Madam,

I beg to remain,

Your obedient servant,

Less formally   Dear Madam,

Yours faithfully,

Socially   Dear Dame Matilda Johnson, *or*

Dear Dame Matilda,

Yours sincerely,

Envelope

Dame Matilda Johnson, GCB (or DCB)

Where the recipient of this honour already enjoys a higher title, either by birth or marriage, the accepted rule would seem to be that for a peeress, or the daughter of a duke, marquess, or earl, her title in this order is indicated only by the letters following her name; that the prefix 'The Hon.' should be used with and preceding 'Dame' (as with a knight); and that the wives or widows of baronets and knights may themselves choose whether they wish to be known as, e.g. Lady Jones, DCG, or Dame Bronwen Jones, DCB.

The Most Distinguished Order of St Michael and St George

There are three classes in this order, for which women as well as men are eligible. Members of the first two classes only are knights or dames, and the use of the title in speech and writing is the same as for baronets and their wives and children (except, of course, for the abbreviation Bt).

Husbands of ladies raised to any one of the ranks in this order do not share their wives' distinctions.

MEN	**Knights**	
	Knights Grand Cross	Sir Robert Johnson, GCMG
	Knights Commanders	Sir Edward Thompson, KCMG
	Companions	Richard Jackson, Esq., CMG

The wives of companions, as such, have no distinctions, though they have recognised precedence.

WOMEN   **Dames**

The title carried by the first two degrees of this order is used always in conjunction with the lady's forename.

	Dames Grand Cross	Dame Matilda Johnson, GCMG
	Dames Commanders	Dame Pamela Thompson, DCMG

Husbands of ladies raised to any of the ranks in this order do not share their wives' distinctions.

In speech   The formal mode of address is 'Dame Matilda' or 'Dame Pamela'.

In writing   *Letter*

Formally   Madam,

I beg to remain,

Your obedient servant,

Less formally   Dear Madam,

Yours faithfully,

Socially   Dear Dame Matilda Johnson, *or*

Dear Dame Matilda,

Yours sincerely,

Envelope

Dame Matilda Johnson, GCMG (or DCMG)

Companions   Mrs Jackson, CMG

The Royal Victorian Order

There are five classes in this order, for which women as well as men are eligible. Members of the first two classes only are knights or dames, and the use of the title in speech and writing (except, of course, for the abbreviation Bt) is the same as for baronets and their wives and children. The wives of commanders and members, as such, have no distinctions, though they have recognised precedence.

Husbands of ladies raised to any one of the ranks in this order do not share their wives' distinctions.

MEN	Knights	
	Knights Grand Cross	Sir Robert Johnson, GCVO
	Knights Commanders	Sir Edward Thompson, KCVO
	Commanders	Richard Jackson, Esq., CVO
	Lieutenants	Charles White, Esq., LVO
	Members	Herbert Black, Esq., MVO
WOMEN	Dames	
	Dames Grand Cross	Dame Matilda Johnson, GCVO
	Dames Commanders	Dame Pamela Thompson, DCVO
	Commanders	Mrs Jackson, CVO
	Lieutenants	Mrs Black, LVO
	Members	Miss Brown, MVO

The Most Excellent Order of the British Empire

This order is the most recent, and women as well as men are eligible.

Members of the first two classes only are knights or dames, and the use of the title in speech and writing (except, of course, the abbreviation Bt) is the same as for baronets and their wives and children. The wives of commanders, officers, and members, as such, have no distinctions, though they have recognised precedence.

Husbands of ladies raised to any one of the ranks in this order do not share their wives' distinctions.

MEN	Knights	
	Knights Grand Cross	Sir Robert Johnson, GBE
	Knights Commanders	Sir Edward Thompson, KBE
	Commanders	Richard Jackson, Esq., CBE

	Officers	Herbert Black, Esq., OBE
	Members	Thomas Brown, Esq., MBE
WOMEN	Dames	
	Dames Grand Cross	Dame Matilda Johnson, GBE
	Dames Commanders	Dame Pamela Thompson, DBE
	Commanders	Mrs Jackson, CBE
	Officers	Mrs Black, OBE
	Members	Miss Brown, MBE

Knights Bachelor

This is the lowest order of knighthood, and is designated thus:

Sir William Jones

that is, with forename (not initials) and surname preceded by the title Sir.

Only in formal documents is the word Knight or the abbreviation Kt sometimes added to the name.

It is never correct to use the letters KB to signify a Knight Bachelor. In all other respects the use of the title in speech and writing (except, of course, the abbreviation Bt) is the same as for baronets and their wives and children (*see* pages 48 to 51).

Widows of Knights

No change is made; they continue to be known as Lady . . . .

Widows of Knights Re-marrying, and Former Wives of Knights

See under **Baronets** (page 50).

Honorary Orders of Knighthood

See under **Baronets** (page 48).

These are conferred from time to time on foreigners. Except in rare cases granted specially by the Sovereign, the recipient has no right to the title of Sir and it should not be used before the name; but the letters signifying membership of an order may be used after the name, without the abbreviation Hon., e.g.

Mr Albert C. Gould, KBE.

The press often refers to 'Sir Bob Geldof' but, being Irish, his KBE is honorary and so he is not entitled to use the title 'Sir'.

Knighthoods in Orders not Bestowed by the Crown

There are a number of orders of chivalry worldwide which may have military, papal or royal origins. Knighthoods in these orders do not confer any title.

Although appointments in the Most Venerable Order of the Hospital of St John of Jerusalem are gazetted, knights and dames in the order do not receive the accolade. The letters GCStJ, KStJ and DStJ are not used after the name. Papal knighthoods in the orders of St Gregory the Great and St Sylvester also do not confer titles, nor do knighthoods in the Sovereign Military Order of Malta; the abbreviations sometimes seen (GCSG, KSG, KSS, KM, for example) should equally not be used after the name.

General Remarks

All the letters signifying membership of orders, and all decorations, should be used in addressing, subject to the point made below, that a lower rank in an order is absorbed in a higher. These letters are shown in the correct order on page 151.

In the case of a Knight Bachelor being also a companion in another order, his designation would be:

Sir Henry Jones, CB

In this case the letters KCB would be wrong, because, although a knight and a member of the Order of the Bath, he is not a knight in that particular order.

When a member of an order of knighthood is promoted to a higher rank within the same order, the lower rank is absorbed in the higher and therefore the designation of the lower rank is omitted after the name. Thus when Richard Jackson, Esq., CVO, is created a knight of the Royal Victorian Order he becomes Sir Richard Jackson, KCVO.

When a son of a viscount or baron or the younger son of an earl receives a knighthood, the foregoing rules apply, except as to the address of envelopes, which should be:

> The Hon. Sir William Browning, KCMG (or otherwise)

> The Hon. Lady Browning

New Titles

All persons awarded orders, decorations and medals may add the appropriate letters to their names immediately after the announcement in the *London Gazette*, e.g.

> John Smith, Esq., CBE

> Major Evan Jones, MC

> Corporal William Brown, MM

Knights Grand Cross and Knights Commanders of Orders of Chivalry and Knights Bachelor may use the prefix 'Sir' immediately after the official announcement in the *London Gazette*.

Ladies who are appointed Dames Grand Cross or Dames Commanders of Orders of Chivalry may assume the prefix 'Dame' as soon as the notice appears in the *London Gazette*.

The appointment of a Knight or Dame is complete when the accolade is bestowed by the Sovereign. In very rare cases, where personal investiture is impracticable, Letters Patent granting full privileges of the honour are issued.

For procedure in the case of new peerages, *see also* page 9.

SCOTTISH CLANS AND TERRITORIAL HOUSES

The heads of large family groupings are known as Chiefs of Clans (Highlands) or Chiefs of Names (Lowlands), named after a common ancestor who founded the clan. Branch chiefs are known as chieftains, and lairds are owners of a Scottish estate. All are under the jurisdiction of the Lord Lyon King of Arms.

By Scots law and custom chiefs of Scottish Clans and Names, chieftains and lairds are known by chiefly styles or territorial designations which are legally part of the surname. Mr is not used and Esq. seldom.

Chiefs and Chieftains

Examples   Mackvicular of Mackvicular is called Mackvicular in his own territorial district or gathering, and elsewhere The Mackvicular because he is chief of the *whole* Name or Clan.

MacHector of Drimmore is called Drimmore.

In speech	The style is Mackvicular, or Drimmore, *without* Mr . . . whatever the rank of the speaker. Their wives are introduced or announced as:
	Mrs Mackvicular of Mackvicular
	Mrs MacHector of Drimmore
In writing	*Letter*
Formally	Sir, *or*
	Dear Sir,
	Yours faithfully,
	From a Clansman
	Dear Chief,
	Yours faithfully,
Socially	Dear Mackvicular,
	Yours sincerely, *or*
	Dear Drimmore,
	Yours sincerely,

In writing   *Envelope*

The address of envelopes has varied, but since most chiefs were feudal Barons (under Scots law; *see* page 13) who had precedence of ordinary Esquires, the tendency is, again, to omit Esq., and frequently forename, thus:

Examples   The Mackvicular of Mackvicular

MacHector of Drimmore

John Brown of Frenchie

English writers who feel uneasy at the omission of Esq. may use it; in this case it *follows* the clan or territorial designation.

Baronets and Knights

Example   Sir James MacHector of Drimmore

Service Rank

Example   Colonel The Mackvicular, DSO

Any decorations follow the territorial designation.

Wives of Chiefs and Chieftains

Examples   The wife of Mackvicular of Mackvicular would be called Mrs Mackvicular *or* Mrs Mackvicular of Mackvicular.

The wife of MacHector of Drimmore would be called Mrs MacHector.

Wives of chiefs, whether or not they are feudal Barons (under Scots law; *see* page 13) have a legal right to be addressed as Lady if they so wish.

Examples   The Lady Mackvicular *or*

The Lady Drimmore

In writing   *Letter*

Formally   Madam, *or*

Dear Madam,

Yours faithfully,

Socially   Dear Mrs Mackvicular of Mackvicular, *or*

Dear Mrs MacHector of Drimmore,

Yours sincerely,

Envelope

Mrs Mackvicular of Mackvicular *or*

Mrs MacHector of Drimmore

Widows of Chiefs and Chieftains

The widow of a chief or laird continues to use the territorial style and the prefix Dowager may be used in the same circumstances as where it is applied to a Peeress (*see* page 12).

Example   The Dowager Mrs Mackvicular of Mackvicular

Children of Chiefs and Chieftains

The heirs of chiefs and chieftains are addressed in writing with the distinction 'younger', often abbreviated to 'yr', before or after the territorial designation,

Examples   John Mackvicular, younger of Mackvicular

James MacHector of Drimmore, younger

They are also introduced or announced in this way. All unmarried daughters use the title.

Examples   Miss MacHector of Drimmore – for the eldest, and

Miss Jean MacHector of Drimmore – for a younger one

It is not the custom for younger sons to use the title.

Lairds

The old Scottish title of laird (lord) is still freely used in Scotland, both of the chiefs and chieftains described above and of other landed proprietors.

In rural Scotland their wives are often styled Lady, though not legally except in the case of the wives of chiefs.

Local custom retained these titles when 'Mrs' was introduced from England towards the close of the 18th century. Technically the 'madam' retained by wives of Irish chieftains is correct, and a few Scottish ones now use it.

Baronets and Knights

Example   Sir John Brown of Frenchie

Service Rank

Example   Colonel Sir John Brown of Frenchie

PRIVY COUNSELLORS

The Privy Council is a body of advisers to the Sovereign and carries out legislative, administrative and judicial functions. The office of Privy Counsellor is conferred for life, but it is not hereditary. It entitles the holder to the distinction The Right Hon. (in Canada, the Hon.) All members of the British Cabinet must be privy counsellors, but all privy counsellors are not members of the Cabinet. Husbands or wives do not share the title.

In the case of the peerage the office of privy counsellor is not indicated, as in the three lowest grades the title of Right Hon. is already used and in the two highest grades it is assumed to be incorporated in the loftier titles (*see* pages 10–11).

Where there is no other title, the name is preceded by the distinction The Right Hon.

In speech	There is nothing to indicate this rank in the style of addressing, which is according to the holder's rank otherwise.
In writing	*Letter*
	Where there is no other title:
Formally	Sir (*or* Dear Sir),
	I have the honour to be, Sir (*or* Dear Sir),
	Yours faithfully,
	Madam, *or*
	Dear Madam,
	I have the honour to be, Madam (*or* Dear Madam),
	Yours faithfully,
Less formally	Dear Sir,
	Yours faithfully,
	Dear Madam,
	Yours faithfully,

In writing	*Letter*
Socially	Dear Mr Williams,
	Yours sincerely,
	Dear Mrs Johnson,
	Yours sincerely,
	Envelope
	The Right Hon. James Williams

Esq. is not used, nor are initials, only forename and surname. His wife would always be addressed as Mrs Williams.

The Right Hon. Matilda Johnson, omitting Mrs, Miss or Ms.

Her husband would always be addressed as Esq. unless the envelope is addressed to husband and wife jointly, in which case he would be Mr (*see* page 68).

British Navy, Army or Air Force Officers

Envelope

Examples   Admiral The Right Hon. Sir James Smith *or*

Colonel The Right Hon. Henry Jones *or*

Air Vice-Marshal The Right Hon. Sir Josiah Blank

Church dignitaries

Envelope

Examples   The Most Rev. and Right Hon. the Lord Archbishop of Blank

The Right Rev. and Right Hon. the Lord Bishop of Blank

UNTITLED PERSONS

The use of 'Esquire', in the addition of the suffix 'Esq.', for every man who cannot claim a higher title persists in formal situations. It used to be the case that social usage limited its application to those considered to merit it through social standing, membership of one of the professions, possession of a degree from Oxford or Cambridge University, and so on, but by the mid twentieth century it was felt to be courteous in general to use it in all correspondence. A reaction, influenced by usage in the United States and some other English-speaking countries, now leads many writers, especially in business, to prefer the use of Mr.

Whichever style is preferred, it should clearly be used consistently. It should, however, not be used in addressing Quakers, who dislike any form of title.

The title Esquire should never be used in conjunction with any other title, as for instance the prefix Mr.

Example   H. J. Robins, Esq. *or*

Mr H. J. Robins

Women are addressed as Mrs if married, Miss if unmarried, or Ms if it is desired not to specify marital status. When a woman marries she may continue to use her maiden name and should be styled Miss or Ms according to preference. It may be convenient to use Ms if marital status is unknown, but it is advisable to find out which style is preferred.

In speech   The formal manner of address in speech is Sir, and the social manner Mr Robins. His wife or a woman of equal status is called Madam, and referred to as Mrs, Miss or Ms Robins.

In writing   *Letter*

Formally   Sir,

I beg to remain, Sir,

Your obedient servant,

Madam,

I beg to remain, Madam,

Your obedient servant,

In writing   *Letter*

Less formally   Dear Sir,

Socially

Yours faithfully,

Dear Madam,

Yours faithfully,

Dear Mr Robins,

Yours sincerely,

Dear Mrs Robins,

Yours sincerely,

Envelope

Harold Robins, Esq. *or*

H. J. Robins, Esq. *or*

Mr H. J. Robins

Mrs Robins, Mrs Harold Robins *or*

Mrs H. J. Robins

(If the person concerned has two or more forenames, it is preferable to use initials; if one only, the name in full.)

For all other male members of the family the rules are the same; for formal correspondence, envelopes to married women should include their husbands' forename, for instance:

Mrs John Robins

although it is more common in today's usage for a married woman to use her own forename, for instance:

Mrs Mary Robins *or*

Mrs M. A. Robins

Widows and Former Wives of Esquires

If a married woman preferred to include her husband's forename it is wrong to change the form of address on widowhood; Mrs John Robins remains Mrs John Robins when her husband dies and should not be addressed by her own forename unless it is her wish. This error might lead strangers to suppose that her marriage had been dissolved.

A former wife would normally use her own forename. Upon divorce a woman may retain her married surname or assume the surname she used prior to marriage.

Sons of Esquires

Sons bearing the same name or initials as their fathers may be addressed:

Harold Robins, Jnr, Esq.

if this is necessary to avoid confusion.

> There was a Victorian habit of addressing young men of nursery and school age as Master Robins, which seems to have died out. Now the more sensible manner of addressing all boys is simply Harold Robins, until they are old enough for the title Esq.

Daughters of Esquires

The eldest unmarried daughter of the head of the family is Miss Robins. All other unmarried women in the family use their distinguishing forename, for example:

Miss Jane Robins

Orders of Knighthood

Some doubt arises occasionally as to the lesser grades of orders of knighthood. Commanders, Companions, Officers and Members of the various orders of knighthood are addressed as esquires with the distinguishing abbreviation after the name, thus:

Richard Jackson, Esq., CVO

(For fuller details *see under* **Knights** page 52.)

JOINT FORMS OF ADDRESS

It is occasionally necessary to address a letter to married couples or co-habiting partners jointly, such as letters to close friends and relatives. The only difficulty arises where each spouse is entitled to a different form of address; on these occasions it is necessary to distinguish between them:

Mr and Mrs R. F. Jackson

The Lord and Lady Jackson

The Rev. R. F. and Mrs Jackson

Mr R. F. and Rev. Mary Jackson

The Rev. R. F. and Mary Jackson

Sir Richard and Lady Jackson

Mr R. F. and the Hon. Mrs Jackson

Sir Richard Jackson, Bt, and Lady Jackson

The Right Hon. Richard Jackson and Mrs Jackson

Mr R. F. and the Right Hon. Mary Jackson

Mr Richard Jackson and Miss Elizabeth Smith

Mr Richard Jackson and Mr John Smith

Mrs Elizabeth Smith-Jackson and Mrs Jane Smith-Jackson

Where one spouse has honours or decorations indicated by letters after the name these must be shown with the right name:

Colonel R. F. Jackson, CBE, and Mrs Jackson

Sir Richard Jackson and Dame Patricia Jackson, DBE

Mr R. F. Jackson and Dame Mary Jackson, DCMG

Sir Richard Jackson, KBE, and Lady Jackson

See also pages 21, 28, 36, 42 and 47 for the married daughters of peers.

DOUBLE NAMES

The traditional justification for a hyphenated double name has been when two land-owning families have been merged into one through marriage, or when legal licence to adopt it has been obtained. The form can also be applied by those who use a second forename prefixed to the surname for distinction or for convenience, though in such cases a hyphen should not be used. In speech as well as writing the two names are always used.

Upon marriage, while it is traditional for the woman to take the man's surname, it is increasingly common for the woman to keep her maiden name, for professional or identity reasons, or for a married couple to create their own double-barrelled surname by using both of their original surnames. It is personal choice whether a hyphen is used and which order the names are placed.

PRESIDENTS OF SOCIETIES

The presidents of societies are addressed in formal speech and writing as Sir or Mr President. In the case of a titled holder of the office he would be addressed according to his rank, e.g. My Lord Duke (or Your Grace) and President, or My Lord and President, etc. Where a woman holds office she is addressed as Madam President (except that a duchess would be Your Grace and President). In all cases envelopes are addressed according to name and rank, with the addition of:

President of the . . .

GLOSSARY: Religion

Archbishop: a bishop of higher rank.

Archdeacon: a senior clergyman appointed by the bishop to administer part of a diocese.

Archimandrite: a priest in the Eastern Orthodox Church.

Beneficed: an ecclesiastical position that guarantees a fixed income.

Bishop: a senior clergyman in a diocese.

Canon: a cleric who is a member of a cathedral or collegiate church. They can have specific roles within the cathedral (residentiary) or the title can be given because of their service to the diocese (honorary).

Cardinal: a senior cleric in the Roman Catholic Church appointed by a pope to membership of the College of Cardinals.

Clergyman *or* **cleric:** a person who has been ordained.

Coadjutor: an assistant to the bishop.

Dean: a cleric who is appointed to look after the clergy in a defined geographical area or in a cathedral or collegiate church. In some cathedrals they are known as Provosts.

Diocese: a geographical area overseen by a bishop

Metropolitan: a bishop who is head of an ecclesiastical province in the Eastern Orthodox Church.

Monsignori: a title conferred by a pope on high-ranking clerics.

Patriarch: a senior bishop in the Eastern Orthodox Church.

Prebendary: an ancient title which gave senior members of the clergy an income from a piece of land; today it is an honorary post. In some cathedrals, honorary canons are known as prebendaries.

Prelate: a high-ranking member of the clergy in the Roman Catholic Church.

Protonotary: an official in the Roman Catholic Church.

Provincial: a superior of a religious institute with supervision over a territorial area.

Provost: some cathedrals appoint Provosts rather than Deans.

Rabbi: a teacher in a school or spiritual leader of a Synagogue. In the UK the Orthodox Jewish faith is led by the Chief Rabbi of the United Hebrew Congregations of the Commonwealth.

Religious community: a group of people who live together having taken religious vows, for example in a monastery, convent, priory or abbey. The community may follow the rules of a particular order, such as the Order of Saint Benedict. The head of a community is an abbot (male), or abbess, prioress, superior or mother (female).

Suffragan Bishop: an assistant to the bishop.

THE CHRISTIAN CHURCH:
Church of England

The Church of England, the established (state) church in England, is divided into two provinces, Canterbury and York. These are divided into dioceses, which each have a bishop and usually at least one suffragan (assistant) bishop. Each diocese is split into archdeaconries, which are further divided into deaneries, a collection of parishes.

The Church of England is part of the Anglican Communion, an international association of churches where there is mutual agreement on essential doctrines.

Lords Spiritual

The Archbishops of Canterbury and York, the Bishops of London, Durham, Winchester and twenty-one of the other English Diocesan Bishops in order of seniority of consecration constitute the Lords Spiritual in Parliament. The Bishop of Sodor and Man has an honorary seat in the House of Lords but is a member of the House of Keys, Isle of Man.

Archbishops of Canterbury and York

The Archbishop of Canterbury ranks next in precedence to the Royal Family, and above the Lord Chancellor. The Archbishop of York ranks next to the Lord Chancellor, and above dukes.

Signatures

A reigning archbishop uses his forename in English or Latin, or the initials of his forenames, coupled with the Latin name of his see, or some abbreviation of it. (When the abbreviated Latin name of the see is used it is usual to put a colon instead of a full stop.) The Archbishop of Canterbury signs himself (e.g. Thomas) Cantuar:, and the Archbishop of York signs (e.g. Henry) Ebor.

In speech   They are referred to as the Archbishop of Canterbury (or York), and not by name. The manner of addressing by both equals and inferiors is Your Grace.

In writing	*Letter*
Formally	My Lord Archbishop, *or*
	Your Grace,
	I have the honour to remain, my Lord Archbishop,
	Your Grace's devoted and obedient servant,
Less formally	My Lord Archbishop,
	Yours faithfully,
Socially	Dear Lord Archbishop, *or*
	Dear Archbishop,
	Yours sincerely,
In writing	*Envelope*
	The Archbishops of Canterbury and York, being Privy Counsellors, are addressed as:
	The Most Rev. and Right Hon. the Lord Archbishop of Canterbury (*or* York)

'The Reverend' is often abbreviated to 'The Rev.' although some clergymen prefer it to be written in full.

Retired Archbishops of Canterbury and York

It has recently been the custom to bestow a temporal peerage upon a retiring Archbishop of Canterbury or upon a retiring Archbishop of York who does not become Archbishop of Canterbury, e.g. Archbishop Lord Coggan, Archbishop Lord Fisher of Lambeth and Archbishop Lord Blanch. They would otherwise renounce their seats in the House of Lords.

Signatures

Retired Archbishops of Canterbury and York use the name that forms part of their temporal title, e.g. Coggan, Fisher of Lambeth and Blanch – according to the usage for temporal peers.

In speech	They are referred to as Archbishop Lord . . . (see examples above). The manner of addressing is Your Grace or My Lord.
In writing	*Letter*
	Usage is as for reigning archbishops.

Envelope

As Privy Counsellors, they retain the address Right Hon.

The Most Rev. and Right Hon. Lord . . . or

The Right Rev. and Right Hon. Lord . . .

It is necessary to find out which is preferred.

Other Archbishops of the Anglican Communion

Signatures

The Archbishop of Wales signs himself (e.g. Emrys) Cambrensis, the Archbishop of Armagh signs himself (e.g. James) Armagh, and the Archbishop of Dublin signs himself (e.g. Patrick) Dublin.

In speech	They are referred to by their territorial titles, e.g. the Archbishop of . . . , and not by name; but where no confusion is likely, 'the Archbishop' is sufficient. The manner of addressing in speech by both equals and inferiors is Your Grace or My Lord.

In writing   *Letter*

Formally
and socially   As for Canterbury and York

Envelope

All archbishops are addressed, both formally and socially as:

The Most Rev. the Lord Archbishop of . . .

An exception, however, occurs in the case of the Archbishop of Armagh, who is addressed thus:

The Most Rev. His Grace the Lord Primate of All Ireland

Retired Archbishops

On resigning, an archbishop, though relinquishing his legal, constitutional and ecclesiastical status as archbishop, remains a bishop, and should in principle be addressed as Right Reverend rather than Most Reverend. By courtesy, nevertheless (or by habit), he may still be addressed as archbishop; unless, having perhaps held archiepiscopal office overseas, he should be appointed as a bishop in this country, when he will be addressed as a bishop. This will be so if the appointment is as diocesan, suffragan or assistant bishop, according to the rule for each.

Signatures

Retired archbishops use their ordinary signatures, with the addition of Archbishop or Bishop.

In speech	Retired archbishops are referred to in speech, both socially and formally, by title and surname; it is again necessary to discover whether Archbishop, or Bishop, is preferred. The manner of address in conversation is My Lord.
In writing	*Letter*
Formally	My Lord, *or*
	My Lord Bishop, *or*
	My Lord Archbishop (where this form is retained), I have the honour to remain, My Lord (*or* as above),
	Your devoted and obedient servant,
Less formally	My Lord,
	Yours faithfully,
Socially	Dear Lord Bishop, *or*
	Dear Bishop, *or*
	Dear Archbishop,
	Yours sincerely,
	Envelope
	The Right Rev. John Brown *or*
	The Most Rev. John Brown
	There is no alternative to discovering which form is preferred in each case.

Wives of Archbishops

Being a wife of an archbishop confers no precedence or special title. A wife is plain Mrs unless she has a title of her own or her husband has a temporal title.

Bishops

All the bishops of the Anglican Communion have come by custom or right to be styled Lord Bishops and have attracted forms of address of the highest dignity and reverence. Their variable forms have taken their present shape of Lord Bishop, a title which may be used with propriety of all episcopally consecrated bishops. Though in the Eastern churches titles more splendid and picturesque are in use, Lord Bishop is never wrong.

The title 'Lord Bishop' is not confined to those English diocesan bishops who happen by reason of seniority to have seats in the House of Lords. All diocesan bishops of England are described in legal documents as Lord Bishops. The title owes nothing to special grant or to any act of sovereignty by monarch. Nor can the title be traced to the fact that bishops were formerly barons also, possessing land and revenues accordingly. The title *Dominus Episcopus* was in use before the Conquest and before the bishops were constituted barons.

However, the use of 'Lord' before 'Bishop' is diminishing. It is a matter of individual preference whether it should be used.

The twenty-four English bishops who, with the two archbishops, have seats in the House of Lords, rank below viscounts and above barons.

Women in the Church of England

Women were first ordained as priests in 1994. Following legislation adopted by the Church of England in 2014, its first female bishop was consecrated in January 2015 when Rt Rev. Libby Lane became Suffragan Bishop of Stockport. The first female diocesan bishop was Rt Rev. Rachel Treweek, who was consecrated Bishop of Gloucester in July 2015. 'The Lord Bishop' is still the correct designation for a female diocesan bishop.

In speech	The manner of address in speech is My Lord and His Lordship, both formally and socially.
In writing	*Letter*
Formally	My Lord, *or*
	My Lord Bishop,
	I have the honour to remain,
	Your Lordship's obedient servant,
Less formally	My Lord,
	Yours faithfully,

Socially Dear Lord Bishop, *or* Dear Bishop,

     Yours sincerely,

     Envelope

     The Right Rev. the Lord Bishop of . . .

Bishops Suffragan

A Bishop Suffragan is appointed as an assistant to the Diocesan Bishop. In the United Kingdom they are not addressed as 'Suffragan' but by courtesy exactly as diocesan bishops; they are styled Bishop of . . . , not Bishop Suffragan of whatever the diocese may be.

(*Example* The Bishops Suffragan of Grantham and Grimsby are addressed as though they were diocesan bishops of sees of these names, and not as Bishops Suffragan in the diocese of Lincoln.)

In Canada and Australia, however, although they may (particularly in Canada) be given a territorial style of their own, they are thought of and addressed as suffragans of the diocese:

The Right Rev. the Suffragan Bishop of . . .

Bishops of the Anglican Communion

In speech The manner of address in speech and writing, both
and writing formally and socially, is exactly the same as for English
     bishops. There are, however, the following minor points
     of distinction to be borne in mind.

Irish Bishops

In speech The manner of address in speech and writing is the
and writing same as for English bishops.

     The exception is the Bishop of Meath, who is addressed
     as 'The Most Rev.' instead of 'The Right Rev.', as
     Premier Bishop of the Church of Ireland.

Scottish Bishops

The same as for Irish bishops (*see above*). One bishop is elected as Primus who is addressed In speech and writings as 'My Lord' or 'My Lord Primus'.

In writing *Envelope*

     The Most Rev. the Primus

Elsewhere

In speech and writing	Some bishops discourage the use of the title – this is their preference. Until lately the title has been unknown in the American Episcopal Church, so far as domestic use is concerned, but American bishops should in courtesy be addressed by English-speaking correspondents outside the USA in the manner applicable to all other bishops of the Anglican Communion. The American style 'Right Reverend Sir' is, indeed, giving place occasionally to 'My Lord' in USA.

Bishops Coadjutor

In speech and writing	In the Anglican Church overseas Bishops Coadjutor may be appointed to assist an Archbishop. They have no separate territorial style, and are addressed by name, with the addition of their office:

The Right Rev. A. B. . . . , Bishop Coadjutor of . . .

Assistant Bishops

In speech and writing	In Britain Assistant Bishops may be appointed, after retirement as a diocesan or suffragan, to assist the bishop of the diocese in which they are living. They are addressed by name. In the Anglican church overseas this title may be given to younger men who after consecration are appointed to assist the bishop of a large diocese. The form of address is the same in either case:

The Right Rev. C. D. . . .

Retired Bishops

In speech	Retired bishops are addressed by their names, but otherwise as for English bishops.
In writing	*Letter*
Formally and socially	As for English bishops
	Envelope
	The Right Rev. John Brown

Wives of Bishops

As for the wives of archbishops, no precedence or special title is conferred. A wife is plain Mrs unless she has a title of her own or her husband has a temporal title.

Deans

In speech	The style of address is Dean.
In writing	*Letter*
Formally	Very Reverend Sir *or* Madam
	I have the honour to remain, Very Reverend Sir *or* Madam,
	Your obedient servant,
Less formally	but on a church matter:
	Dear Sir *or* Madam,
	Yours faithfully,
Socially	Dear Dean,
	Yours sincerely,
	Envelope
	The Very Rev. the Dean of . . .
	Deans who are also Bishops are addressed as The Right Rev. the Dean of . . .

Retired Deans

Retired deans have no right to the title on retirement, and are addressed as other members of the clergy (*see* page 83), but if the title Dean Emeritus is conferred they are addressed as deans (also, by courtesy, if it is known that they wish to retain the title), except that the envelope would be addressed in the personal name, thus:

The Very Rev. Charles Cox

Provosts

Provosts are the incumbents of those parish churches which have become cathedrals in recent times. They take rank and precedence as deans.

In speech	They are addressed as Provost.

In writing	*Letter*
Formally	Very Reverend Sir *or* Madam,
	I have the honour to remain, Very Reverend Sir *or* Madam,
	Your obedient servant,
Less formally	but on a church matter:
	Dear Sir *or* Madam,
	Yours faithfully,
Socially	Dear Provost,
	Yours sincerely,
	Envelope
	The Very Rev. the Provost of . . .

Retired Provosts

Rules as for retired deans apply.

Archdeacons

In speech	They are addressed as Archdeacon.
In writing	*Letter*
Formally	Venerable Sir *or* Madam,
	I have the honour to remain, Venerable Sir *or* Madam,
	Your obedient servant,
Less formally	but on a church matter:
	Dear Sir *or* Madam,
	Yours faithfully,
Socially	Dear Archdeacon,
	Yours sincerely,
	Envelope
	The Venerable the Archdeacon of . . .

Retired Archdeacons

Retired archdeacons have no right to the title on retirement, and are addressed as other members of the clergy (*see* page 83), but if the title

Archdeacon Emeritus is conferred on them (also, by courtesy, if it is known that they wish to retain the title), they are addressed in speech as Archdeacon and referred to as Archdeacon . . . (surname), except in official documents. The envelope would be addressed:

The Venerable Arthur Holt

Canons

Canons are either residentiary or honorary. The rule is the same in each case.

In speech	They are addressed as Canon . . . (surname).
In writing	*Letter*
Formally	Reverend Sir *or* Madam,
	I have the honour to remain, Reverend Sir *or* Madam,
	Your obedient servant,
Less formally	but on a church matter:
	Dear Sir *or* Madam,
	Yours faithfully,
Socially	Dear Canon, *or*
	Dear Canon . . . (surname),
	Yours sincerely,
	Envelope
	The Rev. Canon . . . (forename and surname)

Minor canons are addressed as other members of the clergy, with no special title.

Prebendaries

In speech	Prebendaries are addressed as Prebendary . . .
In writing	*Letter*
Formally	Reverend Sir *or* Madam,
	I have the honour to be, Reverend Sir *or* Madam,
	Your obedient servant,
Less formally	but on a church matter:
	Dear Sir *or* Madam,
	Yours faithfully,

Socially   Dear Prebendary, *or*

               Dear Prebendary . . . ,

               Yours sincerely,

               Envelope

               The Rev. Prebendary . . .

Other Members of the Clergy

There is no difference in style of addressing the remaining ranks, although beneficed clergy are usually called in speech either The Rector or The Vicar. But it is definitely wrong to refer or write to the Rev. Smith. Initials or forename must always be used, unless they are not known.

The style Rev. Mr Smith was once common in England but its use is now confined to North America, where it is correct.

In speech   They are addressed as Vicar, Rector or Mr or Mrs, Miss
                  . . .

In writing   *Letter*

Formally   Reverend Sir/Madam, *or*

                  Sir/Madam,

                  I beg to remain, Reverend Sir/Madam (*or* Sir/Madam),

                  Your obedient servant,

Less formally   Dear Sir *or* Madam,

                  Yours faithfully,

Socially   Dear Mr *or* Mrs, Miss Smith, *or*

                  Dear Rector (or Vicar),

                  Yours sincerely,

                  Envelope

                  The Rev. A. B. Smith

                  When the name of a member of the clergy and his or her spouse appear together, the correct form is:

                  The Rev. A. B. and Mrs Smith *or* Mr A. B. and Rev. Mary Smith

Titled Clerics

A temporal title is always preceded in writing by the spiritual one.

Examples   The Right Rev. and Right Hon. the Lord Bishop of London

The Rev. Lord John Smith

The Rev. The Hon. David Jones

The Rev. Sir John Bull, Bt

No ordained priest of the Church can receive the accolade of knighthood, but in some cases an appointment to an order of knighthood is made which carries the designation (e.g. KCVO) without the title. The initials follow the name in the usual way:

The Right Rev. John Brown, KCVO

or, where the see rather than the name is used:

The Right Rev. the Lord Bishop of . . . , KCVO

The wife of a priest so honoured is not styled or addressed Lady unless she is already entitled to such designation.

Anglican Religious Communities

MEN	**Head of Community**
In speech	Father Abbot *or* Father Prior *or* Father Superior
In writing	*Letter*
	Dear Abbot (*or* Prior *or* Superior),
	Yours faithfully,
	Envelope
	The Right Rev. the Lord Abbot *or*
	The Rev. the Prior *or*
	The Rev. (*or* The Rev. Father) Superior
	The initials of the Community (should it use them) are added immediately after the name, even if there are decorations or degrees as well.
	Ordained Members of a Community
In speech	Father *or* (in Franciscan Communities) Brother
In writing	*Letter*
	Dear Rev. Father,
	Yours faithfully,

Envelope

The Rev. (*or* The Rev. Father) A. B. Smith, SSJE

The Rev. (*or* The Rev. Father) J. L. Read, CR, DD

Lay Members of Community

In speech	Brother John
In writing	*Letter*
	Dear Brother John,
	Yours faithfully,
	Envelope
	Brother John Green

Benedictines

Whether ordained or lay, Benedictines are addressed as Dom:

The Rev. Dom James Martin, OSB *or*

Dom James Martin, OSB, if a lay member

WOMEN	**Head of Community**
In speech	Reverend Mother (in some Communities, Mother *or* Sister
In writing	*Letter*
	Dear Reverend Mother *or* Sister,
	Yours faithfully,
	Envelope
	The Rev. The Prioress *or*
	The Rev. Mother Superior
	Ordinary Members of Community
In speech	Sister Mary
In writing	*Letter*
	Dear Sister Mary,
	Yours faithfully,
	Envelope
	Sister Mary Brown
	followed by the initials of the Community.

Benedictines

Benedictines are addressed as Dame:

Dame Mary Brown, OSB

Chancellors

Chancellors are the judges of the Episcopal Courts and the principal lay officers of the respective dioceses. They are usually, but not invariably, barristers. The title is used only in connection with official duties.

In speech	By the clergy and others within the diocese:
	Mr Chancellor, *or more familiarly*
	Chancellor
	Madam Chancellor
	In court:
	Sir, Worshipful Sir (not Your Worship) and The Learned Chancellor are correct.
	Madam, Worshipful Madam
In writing	*Letter*
Formally	Sir (*or* Dear Sir),
	Madam (*or* Dear Madam),
Less formally	Dear Mr Chancellor,
	Dear Madam Chancellor,
	Envelope
	The Worshipful Chancellor Smith *or*
	The Worshipful Thomas Smith *or*
	The Worshipful Sir Thomas Smith (if a knight)
	The Worshipful Alice Jones *or*
	The Worshipful Lady Alice Jones (if a dame)
	If the chancellor is a QC the initials should come after the name.

Chancellors of Cathedrals

Chancellors of cathedrals are clergymen and should be addressed by clerical title.

THE CHRISTIAN CHURCH:
Church of Scotland

The Church of Scotland (the Kirk) dates from 1690 and is organised into courts, the highest of which is the General Assembly. Meetings of the Assembly are chaired by the Moderator and observed by the British Sovereign's representative, the Lord High Commissioner.

The Lord High Commissioner to the General Assembly

In speech	He or she is addressed and referred to as Your Grace and His or Her Grace. Only during the term of office is he or she entitled to any special form of address.
In writing	*Letter*
Formally	Your Grace,
and socially	Your Grace's most devoted and obedient servant,
	When the office is held by a member of the Royal Family, the formal and social address may be either Your Royal Highness or Your Grace.
	Envelope
	His *or* Her Grace the Lord High Commissioner

The Moderator

In speech	He or she is addressed as Moderator, *or* as Dr . . .
	(*or* Mr/Mrs/Miss/Ms . . . , as the case may be).
In writing	*Letter*
Formally	Right Reverend Sir/Madam,
	I beg to remain, Right Reverend Sir/Madam,
	Your obedient servant,
Less formally	Dear Sir/Madam, *or*
	Dear Moderator,
	Yours faithfully,
Socially	Dear Moderator, *or*
	Dear Dr (or Mr/Mrs/Miss/Ms) Smith,
	Yours sincerely,

In writing	*Envelope*
	The Right Rev. the Moderator of the General Assembly of the Church of Scotland

Ex-Moderators

These dignitaries are designated The Very Reverend.

In speech	They are addressed as Dr . . . (*or* Mr/Mrs/Miss/Ms . . .).
In writing	*Letter*
Formally	Very Reverend Sir/Madam,
	I beg to remain, Very Reverend Sir/Madam,
	Your obedient servant,
Less formally	Dear Sir/Madam, *or*
	Dear Minister,
	Yours faithfully,
Socially	Dear Dr (*or* Mr/Mrs/Miss/Ms) Smith,
	Yours sincerely,
	Envelope
	The Very Rev. Albert Smith (and if a Dr), DD.

Other Members of the Clergy

Rules as for the Church of England apply (*see* page 83), except that the titles of Vicar and Rector are not used. A minister in a regular parochial charge is often called The Minister (of the parish) or the Parish Minister, and addressed as Dr . . . (surname) or Mr/Mrs/Miss/Ms . . . (surname). Envelopes are addressed The Minister of . . .

Dean of the Thistle and Chapel Royal

Rules as for Deans of the Church of England apply here (*see* page 80).

THE CHRISTIAN CHURCH:
Roman Catholic Church

The Roman Catholic Church is a worldwide group of churches in communion with the Bishop of Rome (the Pope).

It should be understood that the following rules have no legal foundation in the UK. Roman Catholic archbishops and bishops have no claim to territorial titles or to the use of the salutations Your Grace or My Lord, and such modes of address are not permitted in official documents and circles. However, unofficially and within the Roman Catholic community these styles are used.

The Pope

The Pope is the supreme head on earth of the Roman Catholic Church.

In speech	He is personally addressed and referred to as Your Holiness or His Holiness.
In writing	*Letter*
Formally	Your Holiness,
	I have the honour to remain,
	Your Holiness's most devoted and obedient child,
	or
	Most Holy Father,
	Your Holiness's most humble child,
	A non-Roman Catholic may subscribe himself 'servant' and not 'child'.
	Envelope
	His Holiness The Pope
	Letters addressed to the Pope would normally go through ecclesiastical channels, and if written in English would be translated into Latin.

Cardinals

In speech	Cardinals are addressed and referred to both formally and socially as Your Eminence and His Eminence.

In writing	*Letter*
Formally	My Lord Cardinal, *or*
	Your Eminence,
	I have the honour to remain, my Lord Cardinal,
	Your Eminence's devoted and obedient child,
	A non-Roman Catholic may subscribe himself 'servant' and not 'child'.
Less formally	Your Eminence,
	I remain, Your Eminence,
	Yours faithfully,
Socially	Dear Cardinal . . . ,
	Yours sincerely,
	Envelope
	His Eminence Cardinal . . .

Cardinal Archbishops and Cardinal Bishops

Rules as for Cardinals apply here, except as to the address of envelope, which should be:

His Eminence the Cardinal Archbishop of . . .

or, preferably

His Eminence Cardinal . . . , Archbishop of . . .

since the dignity of Cardinal is personal, and not attached to the office of Archbishop. The same rule should be followed for Cardinals who are Bishops.

Archbishops

In speech	Archbishops are addressed and referred to in speech both formally and socially as Your Grace and His Grace.
In writing	*Letter*
Formally	My Lord Archbishop, *or*
	Your Grace,
	I have the honour to remain, my Lord Archbishop,
	Your Grace's devoted and obedient child,

A non-Roman Catholic may subscribe himself 'servant' and not 'child'.

Less formally	Your Grace,
	Yours faithfully,
Socially	Dear Archbishop,
	Yours sincerely,

Envelope

His Grace The Archbishop of . . . *or*

The Most Rev. James Smith, Archbishop of . . .

The Archbishop of Armagh is the Primate of All Ireland, and the Archbishop of Dublin is the Primate of Ireland. In these cases the following form is appropriate:

The Most Rev. James Smith

Archbishop of Armagh and Primate of All Ireland

The Most Rev. James Smith

Archbishop of Dublin and Primate of Ireland

Form used within British Commonwealth

In writing	*Letter*
	Most Reverend Sir,
	I (We) have the honour to be,
	Your faithful servant(s),
	Envelope
	The Most Rev. Archbishop Brown

Retired Archbishops

| In writing | *Envelope* |
| | The Most Rev. Archbishop Smith |

Bishops

In speech	The manner of address both formally and socially is My Lord and His Lordship.
In writing	*Letter*
Formally	My Lord, *or*

My Lord Bishop,

I have the honour to remain,

Your Lordship's obedient child (or servant),

Less formally   My Lord,

Yours faithfully,

Socially   Dear Bishop,

Yours sincerely,

Envelope

The Right Rev. James Smith, Bishop of . . . *or*

His Lordship the Bishop of . . .

Form used within British Commonwealth

In writing   *Letter*

Right Reverend Sir,

I (We) have the honour to be,

Your faithful servant(s),

Envelope

The Right Rev. Bishop Brown

Irish Bishops

The foregoing rules apply, except that the envelope is addressed:

The Most Rev. the Bishop of . . .

Other English-Speaking Countries

Bishops in other English-speaking countries are customarily also addressed as Most Rev.

Retired Bishops

In writing   *Envelope*

The Right Rev. Bishop Smith

Bishops Coadjutor

In speech   Bishops Coadjutor are appointed to assist a bishop or
and writing   archbishop, and will normally succeed him on his
retirement. They are addressed as bishops, but are

referred to and addressed on envelopes by personal name.

Example   The Right Rev. William Flynn, Bishop Coadjutor of . . .

Bishops Auxiliary

In speech and writing	Bishops Auxiliary are also appointed to assist an archbishop or a bishop, but without the expectation of succession. They are addressed as bishops, but are referred to and addressed on envelopes by personal name.

Example   The Right Rev. John Haines, Bishop Auxiliary of . . .

Titular Sees

A titular see is an honorary title for a bishop who has no see or an honorary additional title for a bishop who has one.

In writing	Foregoing rules for Archbishops and Bishops apply, except as to envelopes, which are addressed:

The Most Rev. Archbishop Brown

The Right Rev. (*or* Most Rev.) Bishop Brown

It is unnecessary to refer to the titular see.

Provosts

In speech	They are addressed as Provost . . .
In writing	*Letter*
Formally	Very Reverend Sir,
	I have the honour to remain, Very Reverend Sir,
	Your obedient servant,
Less formally	Dear Sir,
	Your faithfully,
Socially	Dear Provost . . . , *or*
	Dear Provost,
	Yours sincerely,

Envelope

The Very Rev. Provost . . .

Canons

In speech   Canons are addressed and referred to as Canon . . .

In writing   *Letter*

Formally   Very Reverend Sir,

I have the honour to remain, Very Reverend Sir,

Your obedient servant,

Less formally   Dear Sir,

Yours faithfully,

In writing   *Letter*

Socially   Dear Canon . . . , *or*

Dear Canon,

Yours sincerely,

Envelope

The Very Rev. Canon . . .

If he is a Monsignore, this is added: The Very Rev. Monsignor (Canon) . . . . Both titles may be used, but it is unnecessary.

Monsignori

Monsignori may be Protonotaries, Domestic Prelates, Privy Chamberlains, or Honorary Chamberlains of His Holiness the Pope.

In speech   They are addressed and referred to both formally and socially, as Monsignor Smith, or as Monsignore.

In writing   *Letter*

Formally   Reverend Sir,

I have the honour to remain, Reverend Sir,

Your devoted and obedient servant,

Less formally   Reverend Sir,

Yours faithfully,

Socially	Dear Monsignore, *or*
	Dear Monsignor Smith,
	Yours sincerely,
	Envelope
	The Rev. Mgr Vincent Smith, *or*
	The Rev. Monsignore

Priests

In speech	Priests are addressed and referred to as Father . . .
In writing	*Letter*
Formally	Dear Reverend Father,
	Your devoted and obedient child (or servant),
Less formally	Dear Reverend Father,
	Yours faithfully,
Socially	Dear Father . . . ,
	Yours sincerely,
	Envelope
	The Rev. Father . . .

Titled Priests

As with the clergy of the Church of England (*see* page 84), the spiritual title always precedes the temporal one.

Roman Catholic clergy do, however, use the title Sir if they become a member of an order of knighthood; the former Archbishop of Sydney, for example, was known as His Eminence Sir Norman Cardinal Gilroy, KBE.

Roman Catholic Religious Communities

Provincials

In speech	Provincials are addressed and referred to as Father . . .
In writing	*Letter*
Formally	Very Reverend Father,
	I beg to remain, Very Reverend Father,
	Your devoted and obedient child (or servant),

Less formally	Very Reverend Father,
	Yours faithfully,
In writing	*Letter*
Socially	Dear Father . . . , *or*
	Dear Father Provincial,
	Yours sincerely,
	Envelope
	The Very Rev. Father . . . , *or*
	The Very Rev. Father Provincial (with distinguishing initials of his order)

MEN	**Heads of Community: Abbots**
In speech	Abbots are addressed and referred to as Father Abbot.
In writing	*Letter*
Formally	My Lord Abbot, *or*
	Right Reverend Abbot . . . , *or*
	Right Reverend Father,
	I beg to remain, my Lord Abbot (or alternatives),
	Your devoted and obedient servant,
Less formally	My Lord Abbot,
	Yours faithfully,
Socially	Dear Father Abbot,
	Yours sincerely,
	Envelope
	The Right Rev. the Abbot of Thornton (with distinguishing initials of his order)
	Benedictine Abbots do not use the designation 'Lord Abbot'.

Ordained Members of Community

See **Priests** on page 95.

Lay Members of Community

Lay members are addressed as Brother . . . .

Benedictines

Whether ordained or lay, Benedictines are addressed as Dom:

In writing   *Envelope*

The Rev. Dom Henry Smith, OSB *or*

Dom Henry Smith, OSB, if a lay member

WOMEN   **Heads of Community**

The head of a Community may be called Abbess, Prioress, Superior or Reverend Mother.

In speech   She should be addressed as Reverend Mother if not established otherwise.

In writing   *Letter*

Dear Lady Abbess,

Dear Reverend Mother,

Dear Sister Superior,

Yours faithfully,

Envelope

She will be addressed according to her office, with the addition of the letters of her order:

The Lady Abbess

The Reverend Mother Prioress

The Reverend Mother

The Mother Superior

The Sister Superior

Other Members of Community

In speech   and writing   Other members of the order are addressed as The Reverend Sister, with forename, or Christian and surname, according to the custom of the order and, on an envelope, with the letters of the order, if used.

Benedictines

Benedictines are addressed as Dame: Dame Margaret Jones, OSB

THE CHRISTIAN CHURCH:
Free Churches and Other Denominations

A 'free church' is a Christian denomination which is separate from the established or state church.

Ministers

In speech	Ministers are addressed as Dr . . . (*or* Mr . . . , *or* Mrs . . . , *or* Miss . . .).
In writing	*Letter*
Formally	Dear Sir, *or*
	Dear Madam, *or*
	Dear Minister,
	Yours faithfully,
Socially	Dear Dr (*or* Mr, Mrs, or Miss) Smith,
	Yours sincerely,
	Envelope
	The Rev. Matthew Smith *or*
	The Rev. Margaret Smith
	'The Rev. Smith' is in all cases incorrect, and 'Rev. Smith' even more so.

Retired Ministers and Other Clergy

The form of address is the same as for Ministers but without the term Minister being used.

THE CHRISTIAN CHURCH:
Eastern Church

The Eastern Orthodox Church is a communion of self-governing regional Christian churches. The highest ranking bishops are Patriarchs, followed by Metropolitans, Archbishops, Bishops and Archimandrites.

Patriarchs

In speech   Patriarchs are personally addressed and referred to as Your Holiness or His Holiness.

In writing   *Letter*

Your Holiness,

I have the honour to be, Sir,

Your Holiness's obedient servant,

Envelope

His Holiness The Patriarch

Metropolitans

In speech   Metropolitans are personally addressed and referred to as Your Grace and His Grace.

In writing   *Letter*

Your Grace,

I am, Sir,

Your Grace's obedient servant,

Envelope

His Beatitude The Metropolitan of . . .

Archbishops and Bishops

As for Anglican Archbishops and Bishops (*see* pages 73 and 77).

Archimandrites

In speech   Archimandrites are addressed and referred to in speech as Right Reverend Father.

In writing	*Letter*
Formally	Right Reverend Father,
	I beg to remain, Right Reverend Father,
	Your obedient servant,
Socially	Dear Father,
	Yours sincerely,
	Envelope
	The Right Rev. Father . . .

THE JEWISH SYNAGOGUE

The Chief Rabbi

In speech   He is addressed and referred to as Chief Rabbi.

In writing   *Letter*

Formally   Very Reverend and dear Sir,

I am, Very Reverend Sir,

Your obedient servant,

Less formally   Dear Sir,

Yours faithfully,

Socially   Dear Chief Rabbi,

Yours sincerely,

Envelope

The Very Rev. the Chief Rabbi *or*

The Chief Rabbi Dr J. A. Cohen

Rabbis

In speech   Rabbis are addressed and referred to in speech as Rabbi Cohen.

In writing   *Letter*

Formally   Reverend and dear Sir *or* Madam,

I am, Reverend Sir,

Your obedient servant,

Less formally   Dear Sir *or* Madam,

Yours faithfully,

Socially   Dear Rabbi Cohen,

Yours sincerely,

Envelope

The Rev. Rabbi A. D. Cohen

Rabbi Doctors

In speech   Rabbi Doctors are addressed and referred to as Dr Cohen.

In writing	*Letter*
Formally	Dear Sir or Madam,
	Yours faithfully,
Socially	Dear Dr Cohen,
	Yours sincerely,
	Envelope
	The Rev. Rabbi Dr A. D. Cohen

Ministers

In speech	Ministers are addressed and referred to as Mr, Mrs or Miss Cohen or Dr Cohen, according to degree.
In writing	*Letter*
Formally	Reverend and dear Sir *or* Madam,
	I am, Reverend Sir *or* Madam,
	Your obedient servant,
Less formally	Dear Sir,
	Yours faithfully,
Socially	Dear Mr, Mrs, Miss (*or* Dr) Cohen,
	Yours sincerely,
	Envelope
	The Rev. A. D. Cohen *or*
	The Rev. Dr A. D. Cohen

OTHER FAITHS

Many faiths are now practised for which no indisputable body of conventions exists in the United Kingdom. Muslims, Hindus, Sikhs, Buddhists and adherents of other religions have a variety of religious and cultural organisations which have different hierarchies.

It is recommended that an approach be made to places of worship or to cultural centres to ascertain the modes deemed most appropriate for individual priests, ministers and officials.

THE ARMED FORCES:
Comparative Ranks

Royal Navy	Royal Marines	Army	Royal Air Force
Admiral of the Fleet	Captain General	Field Marshal	Marshal of the Royal Air Force
Admiral		General	Air Chief Marshal
Vice Admiral		Lieutenant General	Air Marshal
Rear Admiral	Major General	Major General	Air Vice-Marshal
Commodore RN (senior captains)	Brigadier	Brigadier	Air Commodore
Captain RN	Colonel RM	Colonel	Group Captain RAF
Commander RN	Lieutenant Colonel RM	Lieutenant Colonel	Wing Commander
Lieutenant Commander RN	Major RM	Major	Squadron Leader RAF
Lieutenant RN	Captain RM	Captain	Flight Lieutenant
Sub-Lieutenant RN	Lieutenant RM	Lieutenant	Flying Officer RAF
Midshipman	Second Lieutenant RM	Second Lieutenant	Pilot Officer RAF
Cadet			

Women in the Armed Forces

Women in the Armed Forces used to have ranks of their own, but the Women's Royal Naval Service (WRNS) was integrated into the Royal Navy in 1997; the Women's Royal Army Corps (WRAC) was disbanded in 1992; and the Women's Royal Air Force (WRAF) was merged with the RAF in 1994.

In 2013 Air-Vice Marshal Sue Gray and Air Vice-Marshal Elaine West became the RAF's highest ranking females. In 2015 Major General Susan Ridge became the highest-ranking woman in the Army.

Lieutenant

The pronunciation of 'Lieutenant' in UK and Commonwealth English is 'Lef-tenant'.

THE ARMED FORCES:
Royal Navy

This is the senior fighting service. For all ranks below Rear Admiral, the words Royal Navy, or more usually in ordinary correspondence the abbreviation RN will be added after the name, and any decorations and orders.

Decorations and honours should never be omitted from envelopes.

A few general rules are given below.

In speech	All ranks above that of sub-lieutenant are addressed and referred to by their service title (unless they possess a higher title otherwise).

Admirals of the Fleet

Admirals of the Fleet will normally be holders of some other title.

In writing	*Letter*
	According to peerage or other rank.
	Envelope
Formally and socially	Admiral of the Fleet Lord (or any other title) . . .

Admirals, Vice Admirals, Rear Admirals

In speech	All are addressed as Admiral . . .
In writing	*Letter*
Formally	Sir,
	I have the honour to remain, Sir,
	Your obedient servant,
Less formally	Dear Sir,
	Yours faithfully,
Socially	The social manner is by his title if he has one, otherwise:
	Dear Admiral Flint,
	Yours sincerely,
	Officers of this rank may express a preference for being addressed by rank rather than by title; if so, their preference should be followed.

Envelope

Only on envelopes are the graded service titles used.

The abbreviations Adm., Vice Adm. and Rear Adm. can be used.

Commodores

The rank is held by senior captains in special appointments.

In speech	The title is used with the surname both formally and socially.
In writing	*Letter*
Formally	Sir/Madam,
	I have the honour to be, Sir/Madam,
	Your obedient servant,
Less formally	Dear Sir/Madam,
	Yours faithfully,
Socially	Dear Commodore Beal,
	Yours sincerely,
	Envelope
	Commodore A. N. Beal, Royal Navy (or Cdre A. N. Beal, RN)

Captains

In speech	The title is used with the surname both formally and socially.
In writing	*Letter*
Formally	Sir/Madam,
	I have the honour to be, Sir/Madam,
	Your obedient servant,
Less formally	Dear Sir/Madam,
	Yours faithfully,
Socially	Dear Captain Birch,
	Yours sincerely,

Envelope

Captain A. B. Birch, Royal Navy (or RN)

Commanders

In speech   This title is used with the surname both formally and socially.

In writing   *Letter*

As for Captains, with the title Commander used for social address.

Envelope

Commander C. D. Bartlett, Royal Navy (or RN)

Lieutenant Commanders

In speech   They are addressed as Commander with the surname.

In writing   *Letter*

As for Captains, with the title Commander used for social address.

Envelope (only here is graded title used.)

Lieutenant Commander C. D. Bartlett, Royal Navy (or RN)

Lieutenants

In speech   They are addressed officially as Lieutenant and socially as Mr/Mrs/Miss – both with the surname.

In writing   *Letter*

As for Captains, with the title Lieutenant used for social address.

Envelope

Lieutenant G. H. Crane, Royal Navy (or Lt G. H. Crane, RN)

Sub-Lieutenants, Midshipmen, Cadets

In speech   All are addressed officially and socially as Mr/Mrs/Miss, with the surname.

In writing	*Letter*
	All are addressed as Mr/Mrs/Miss, with the surname.
	Envelope
Formally and socially	Sub-Lieut I. J. Drake, Royal Navy (*or* Sub-Lt I. J. Drake, RN)
	Midshipman K. L. Blake, Royal Navy (*or* RN)
	Cadet M. N. Hawke, Royal Navy (*or* RN)

General List

The foregoing rules apply to all officers on the General List (i.e. Seaman, Engineering, Electrical Engineering, and Supply & Secretariat specialists).

Medical Officers

In speech	Medical Officers should be addressed by rank, prefixed by the name of their branch when referred to.
In writing	*Letter*
	The foregoing rules apply.
	Envelope
	Surgeon Commander S. T. Brice, RN

Chaplains

The Chaplain of the Fleet is an Archdeacon, and is addressed accordingly (*see* page 81) in speech and letter. The envelope may be addressed to The Chaplain of the Fleet, or with this designation added to the name.

Other chaplains are addressed as clergymen with the words Royal Navy or the initials RN attached to their names.

Titled Officers

A hereditary or conferred title is preceded by the naval one.

Examples	Admiral Sir Norman Blake
	Captain the Hon. Norman Birch, Royal Navy (*or* RN)

Retired Officers

A retired officer of the rank of lieutenant commander or above should be addressed in exactly the same way as one of the active list, except that the abbreviation 'Rtd' should be added whenever it is necessary to indicate the fact. For instance, a private letter should be addressed without the suffix, but a letter to a retired officer working, say in the Ministry of Defence, or for a ship-builder, should add 'Rtd'.

Decorations

Abbreviations are used immediately after the name thus:

Captain O. P. Hawke, DSO, Royal Navy

Lieut A. R. Crane, DSC, Royal Navy

They should, of course, never be omitted.

Royal Naval Reserve

Usage is similar to that for professional members of the Royal Navy but forms of address should be employed only on naval business.

THE ARMED FORCES:
Royal Marines

Officers of the Royal Marines have Army ranks although they are more closely connected with the Royal Navy.

In speech   Forms of address are the same as for the Army (*see* pages 112–115).

In writing   *Letter*

Forms of address are the same as for the Army (*see* pages 112–115).

Envelope

The letters RM should follow the surname if the rank is Lieutenant Colonel or below.

Captain General

It will be noted from the table of comparative ranks on page 104 that the highest rank is that of Captain General, and not Field Marshal as in the Army. Any holder of this position will normally possess some other title and will be addressed accordingly.

THE ARMED FORCES:
Army

All ranks above that of lieutenant are addressed and referred to in speech by their service title (unless they possess a higher one otherwise). Decorations and honours should never be omitted from envelopes.

Field Marshals

In speech   Field Marshals will normally be holders of some other title and will be addressed accordingly.

In writing   *Letter*

According to peerage or other rank.

Envelope

Field Marshal Lord (or any other title) . . .

Generals, Lieutenant Generals, Major Generals

In speech   All are addressed as General . . .

In writing   *Letter*

Formally and socially   The formal manner of address is Sir, the social manner is Dear General Sands, or by his title if he has one, according to his preference.

Envelope

Only on envelopes are the graded service titles used.

The abbreviations Gen., Lt Gen. and Maj. Gen. can be used.

Brigadiers

In speech   Brigadiers are addressed by rank and surname, e.g. Brigadier Luttrell.

In writing   *Letter*

Formally   Formal manner of address in writing is Sir/Madam.

Socially   The social manner is Dear Brigadier Luttrell.

Envelope

Brigadier S. B. Luttrell (*or* Brig. S. B. Luttrell)

Colonels

In speech	Colonels are addressed by rank and surname, e.g. Colonel Howe.
In writing	*Letter*
Formally	The formal manner of address in writing is Sir/Madam.
Socially	The social manner, Dear Colonel Howe.
	Envelope
	Colonel F. E. Howe (*or* Col F. E. Howe)

Lieutenant Colonels

In speech	Lieutenant Colonels are addressed by rank and surname, e.g. Colonel Newcombe.
In writing	*Letter*
Formally	The formal manner of address in writing is Sir/Madam.
Socially	The social manner, Dear Colonel Newcombe.
	Envelope
	Only on envelopes is the graded title used. The regiment is added after the name, thus:
	Lieut Colonel H. C. Newcombe, RHA (*or* Lt Col H. C. Newcombe, RHA)

Majors, Captains

In speech	Majors and Captains are addressed by name and rank, e.g. Major Shaw and Captain Shaw.
In writing	*Letter*
Formally	The formal manner of address in writing is Sir/Madam.
Socially	The social manner is Dear Major (or Captain) Shaw.
	Envelope
	Major (or Captain) E. H. Shaw, 11th Hussars

Lieutenants, Second Lieutenants

In speech	Lieutenants are addressed as Mr/Mrs/Miss.
In writing	*Letter*
Formally	The formal manner in writing is Sir/Madam.
Socially	The social manner, Dear Mr/Mrs/Miss Fry.
	Envelope
Official and Service	Lieut (or 2nd Lieut) T. W. Fry, 2nd Life Guards
Socially	T. W. Fry, Esq., 2nd Life Guards *or* Miss T. W. Fry

Medical Officers

Medical Officers should be addressed by rank, pre-fixed by the name of their branch when referred to.

Chaplains

In speech and writing

The Chaplain General to the Forces ranks as major general, and there are four classes below him, ranking respectively as colonels, lieutenant colonels, majors, and captains. In no circumstances however, should military titles be used.

They are all addressed in speech and in writing according to their rank as clergymen. The Chaplain General himself is an Archdeacon.

Envelope

To the Chaplain General of the Forces

Other chaplains have the abbreviation CF or SCF added to their names.

Titled Officers

A hereditary or conferred title is preceded by the military one, as:

Examples	Colonel Lord John Bull, 10th Lancers
	General Sir James Horn

Retired Officers

Retired officers do not have a regiment appended to their names. It used to be the practice for retired officers under the rank of Major to drop their title, but now a retired captain will be addressed by his rank if he chooses to use it.

Decorations

Abbreviations are shown immediately after the name, thus:

Examples   Colonel Newcombe, VC

T. W. Fry, Esq., MC, 2nd Life Guards

They should, of course, never be omitted.

Territorial Army

Usage is similar to that for professional members of the Army but forms of address should be employed only on army business.

THE ARMED FORCES:
Royal Air Force

The rules relating to the Navy and the Army apply in general. All service titles are used officially, but service titles below that of Flight Lieutenant are not used socially. Decorations and honours should never be omitted from envelopes. For ranks below Air Commodore the abbreviation RAF will be added after the name and any decorations and orders. Air Commodores and above are officially graded as 'air officers'.

Marshals of the Royal Air Force

They will normally be holders of some other title, and should be addressed accordingly.

In writing	*Envelope*
	Marshal of the Royal Air Force Lord (or any other title) . . .

Air Chief Marshals, Air Marshals, Air Vice-Marshals

In speech	All are addressed as Air Marshal . . . but the professional title is never further abbreviated.
In writing	*Letter*
Formally	The formal manner of address in writing is Sir/Madam.
Socially	The social manner in writing is Dear Air Marshal (*or* Air Marshal Smith), *or* by his title if he has one, according to his preference.
	Envelope
	Only on envelopes are graded service titles used.

Air Commodores

In speech	Air Commodores are addressed by rank and surname, e.g. Air Commodore Jones.
In writing	*Letter*
Formally	The formal manner of address is Sir/Madam.
Socially	The social manner is Dear Air Commodore Jones.

Envelope

Air Commodore G. H. Jones

The service title is never abbreviated in social usage.

Group Captains, Wing Commanders, Squadron Leaders

In speech	They may be referred to as The Group Captain, *or* Group Captain White *or* addressed as: Squadron Leader *or* Squadron Leader Black
In writing	*Letter*
Formally	The formal manner of address is Sir/Madam.
Socially	The social manner is, e.g. Dear Wing Commander Thomson. *Envelope* Group Captain J. C. White, RAF The service titles are never abbreviated in social usage.

Flight Lieutenants

In speech	Flight Lieutenants are referred to and addressed by rank and surname, e.g. Flight Lieutenant Brown, but not as Flight Lieutenant.
In writing	*Letter*
Formally and socially	The formal and social manner of writing is Flight Lieutenant Brown. *Envelope* Flight Lieutenant Brown The service title is never abbreviated in social usage.

Flying Officers, Pilot Officers

In speech   The service titles are used only for official purposes.
Social manner of address is Mr/Mrs/Miss Gray.

In writing   *Letter*

Formally   The formal manner of writing is Sir/Madam, the social
and socially   manner is Dear Mr/Mrs/Miss Gray.

Envelope

M. B. Gray, Esq., RAF (*or* Miss M. B. Gray, RAF)

Medical Officers

Medical Officers should be addressed by rank, pre-fixed by the name of their branch when referred to.

Chaplains

The Chaplain-in-Chief, Royal Air Force, has the relative rank of Air Vice-Marshal, and other Royal Air Force chaplains have ranks relative to Group Captain down to Flight Lieutenant.

In speech   Chaplains are, however, known and addressed both
officially and otherwise according to their ecclesiastical
titles, which for the Chaplain-in-Chief is Archdeacon,
and not by their relative status in the Royal Air Force.

In writing   *Envelope*

The Reverend A. E. Green, RAF, *not* Squadron Leader
the Rev. A. E. Green.

Titled Officers

A hereditary or conferred title is preceded by the RAF one, as:

Examples   Air Commodore Lord Robert Thomas

Squadron Leader Sir William Evans

Retired Officers

A retired officer who has the rank of Squadron Leader or above should be addressed in exactly the same way as one on the active list, except that the abbreviation 'Rtd' should be added whenever it is necessary to indicate the fact. For instance, a private letter should be addressed without the suffix, but a letter to a retired officer working, say, in the Ministry of Defence should add 'Rtd'.

Decorations

Abbreviations are placed immediately after the name.

Examples   Group Captain J. C. White, DSO, RAF

M. B. Gray, Esq., DFC, RAF

Royal Air Force Volunteer Reserve

Usage is similar to that for professional members of the Royal Air Force but forms of address should be employed only on RAF business.

LAW, DIPLOMATIC AND GOVERNMENT

The various titles and offices are given alphabetically.

Agents-General

These are the representatives in London of the provincial or state government (not the Federal Governments) of Canada or Australia. They are addressed according to their own name and rank, with their office following the name on an envelope.

Aldermen

An Alderman is a high-ranking member of a municipal assembly. This paragraph now applies only to Aldermen of the City of London Corporation and in certain parts of Northern Ireland, since the office has been abolished elsewhere.

In speech	During the term of office an alderman is addressed as Alderman or Madam Alderman.
In writing	*Letter*
Formally	Dear Sir, *or*
	Dear Madam,
Socially	Dear Alderman, *or*
	Dear Alderman Jones, *or*
	Dear Madam Alderman,
	Envelope
	If an Alderman possesses another title this should of course be used; in such cases Alderman precedes other designations; Mr, Mrs or Miss, however, are used before the word Alderman.
	Alderman Sir Joseph Jones
	Mr Alderman Joseph Jones
	Mrs Alderman Jones

Ambassadors

The most senior diplomatic rank, Ambassadors are representatives of the Head of State.

In speech   The formal and social manner of address in speech is Your Excellency *or* Sir *or* Madam.

In writing   *Letter*

Formally   My Lord *or* Lady (or Sir *or* Madam, according to rank),

I have the honour to be, my Lord *or* Lady (or Sir *or* Madam),

Your Excellency's obedient servant,

Socially   Dear Mr *or* Mrs, Miss Whitby (Sir Charles *or* Lady Jane, or according to rank),

Yours sincerely,

Envelope

His Excellency Mr Charles Whitby, CMG (not Esq.) *or*

His Excellency Sir Charles Whitby, KCMG *or*

Her Excellency Mrs Jane Whitby

The form of address for the Apostolic Pro-nuncio is His Excellency, followed by clerical rank.

American ambassadors

The Honorable Charles Whitby

This title is retained for life.

Ambassadors' wives do not share their husbands' official title of Excellency, although it is still accorded them by courtesy in some countries.

Ambassadors' husbands do not share the title of Excellency. They should be addressed according to their own rank or title.

Attorneys-General

The Attorney-General is the chief legal adviser to the Crown.

In speech   Attorneys-General are addressed in speech according to their name and rank. They are invariably QCs and the rules as for Queen's Counsel apply.

In writing   In letters or on envelopes they may be addressed by name and rank or, on the latter, as The Attorney-General.

Bailies (of Scottish Burghs)

A bailie is a civic officer in the local government of Scotland.

In speech   During their term of office they are addressed as Bailie.

In writing   *Letter*

Socially   Dear Bailie Campbell

Envelope

Bailie J. B. Campbell

Chairmen of County Councils

In speech   The Chairman of a County Council is addressed as Mr Chairman, even if the Chairman for the time being is a lady.

In writing   *Envelope*

The Chairman of . . . County Council

Chairmen of District Councils

Since local government reorganisation, cities and towns which once called their civic heads Lord Mayor or Mayor, Lord Provost or Provost in Scotland, have become districts, and their civic heads Chairmen of District Councils. Nevertheless, in those cities and towns which had Mayors or Provosts in the past, the Chairman of the District Council may still be so described, and the forms of address shown under Lord Mayor, Lord Provost, Mayor and Provost still apply (*see* pages 133, 134, 136, 139). Otherwise they are addressed in the same way as Chairmen of County Councils.

Chargés d'affaires

Chargés d'affaires usually take the place temporarily of ambassadors at embassies and of ministers at legations, while at a few posts the office is a permanent one. They rank below envoys-extraordinary (*see* **Ministers** page 137) in diplomatic circles, but the same rules apply.

Circuit Judges

Circuit Judges are appointed to sit in the Crown and County Courts within a specific region of England and Wales.

In speech

Formally and socially	Circuit Judges are addressed and referred to on the Bench as Your Honour and His *or* Her Honour. Socially they are addressed and referred to in conversation as Judge or Judge Jones.
	Where two judges have the same (or even a very similar) surname, the second to be appointed will choose to be known by one of his forenames as well as his surname; for example, Mr Henry Roberts Jones is made a Circuit Judge, and (because there is already a Judge, or a Mr Justice Jones) is known as His Honour Judge Roberts Jones.
In writing	*Letter*
	Dear Judge, *or*
	Dear Judge Jones,
	Yours sincerely,
	Envelope
	His or Her Honour Judge Jones
	Queen's Counsel who are appointed Circuit Judges continue to use the initials QC after their names.

Retired Circuit Judges

The title His/Her Honour is now retained after retirement, omitting the word Judge, and adding the forename or initials; so that the address of Judge Jones on the envelope is:

His Honour Henry Jones

Consuls

A consul is a diplomat, appointed as the head of the consular section of an embassy.

In speech	They are addressed according to name and rank.
In writing	*Letter*
	They are addressed according to name and rank.
	Envelope
	Name should be followed by
	HM Agent and Consul-General *or*
	HM Consul-General *or*
	HM Consul *or*
	HM Vice-Consul

Conveners

The Chairman of a Regional or District Council in Scotland is often known as the Convener or Convenor (both spellings are used).

He (or she) is addressed in the same way as for a Chairman, except that in speech he (or she) is called Convener, without the 'Mr', 'Mrs' or 'Miss'.

Councillors

A Councillor is a member of a local government council.

In speech	During the term of office the manner of address is Councillor.
In writing	*Letter*
Formally	Dear Sir *or* Madam,
Socially	Dear Councillor, *or*
	Dear Councillor Peters,
	Envelope
	Councillor S. N. Peters
	If a Councillor possesses another title this should be used; in such cases Councillor precedes other designations.
	Councillor Sir Stanley Peters

It is better not to add the title Councillor to other titles unless writing on Council business.

Deputy Lieutenants of Counties

Deputy Lieutenants are appointed to support the Lord-Lieutenant.

In speech and writing Deputy Lieutenants are addressed according to their name and rank. When writing to a Deputy Lieutenant in his or her official capacity (and only then), the affix JP should be used (*see* page 149).

District Judges

District Judges are assigned to a particular circuit and deal with cases in the county courts. The same rules are followed as for **Justices of the Peace** (*see* page 141), except that the letters JP are not used for District Judges.

District Judges (Magistrates' Courts)

District Judges (Magistrates' Courts) hear cases in magistrates' courts. The same rules are followed as for **Justices of the Peace** (*see* page 141), except that the letters JP are not used for District Judges.

Envoys-Extraordinary, Ministers-Plenipotentiary

See under **Ministers (Diplomatic Service)**, page 137.

Governors-General, Governors, Lieutenant-Governors

They are appointed to personally represent the Sovereign in a Commonwealth state.

In speech Governors-General and Governors are addressed as 'His *or* Her Excellency' while holding office; the wives of Governors-General are also so addressed, but not the wives of Governors. (Husbands should be addressed according to rank and title.) The Lieutenant-Governors of Jersey, Guernsey, the Isle of Man and Canadian provinces have the same style. For states in Australia see below.

In writing The Governor-General of Canada is called 'Right Honourable' for life. The wife or husband is called 'Her or His Excellency'. The Lieutenant-Governors of Canadian provinces (there are no Governors) are called 'The Honourable' for life, whereas the deputy of the Governor of an Australian state, who is also known as Lieutenant-Governor, is not addressed as 'His or Her Excellency' – or referred to as 'The Honourable' unless already so styled.

Formally	Sir *or* Madam
	I have the honour to be, Sir *or* Madam,
	Your Excellency's obedient servant,
Socially	Dear Governor-General/Governor/Lieutenant-Governor,
	Yours sincerely,
	Envelope
	Her Excellency the Governor-General of . . .
	His Excellency, the Right Hon. Sir John . . . , Governor-General of Canada
	Her Excellency Mrs Christine . . . , Governor of . . .
	His Excellency Mr J. H. . . . , Governor and Commander-in-Chief of (Jersey or Guernsey).

HM Lord-Lieutenants of Counties

(*See* **Lord-Lieutenants of Counties**, page 130)

High Commissioners

High Commissioners represent their country of the Commonwealth in another country.

In speech	They are in effect Ambassadors, and are addressed similarly (*see* page 121).
In writing	*Letter*
Formally	Your Excellency,
	I have the honour to be
	Your Excellency's obedient servant,
Socially	Dear High Commissioner,
	Yours sincerely,

Envelope

His *or* Her Excellency to precede

Mr, Mrs or Miss . . .

The Honourable . . .

The Right Honourable . . .

(according to rank)

Honourable

The title 'Honourable' is accorded in the Commonwealth and other English-speaking countries to holders of a number of public offices, including Ministers (or their equivalent), Judges, members of *some* legislative bodies, Governors or Lieutenant-Governors, and so on. It may be held for life or during tenure of office; within the scope of this book it is sufficient to say that the usage exists and should be followed where it appears; and that it is not usual to abbreviate 'The Honorable' in the United States.

Judges of the High Court

> ### Women in the High Court
>
> In 1965 the first woman Judge of the High Court was appointed, and there are now a number. In 2014 Hon. Dame Alison Russell, unmarried, made history by being the first High Court Judge to be given permission from the Lord Chief Justice to adopt the neutral form 'Hon. Ms Justice' instead of the usual 'Hon. Mrs Justice'.

MEN High Court Judges are usually knighted on appointment.

In speech They are addressed and referred to as My Lord and Your (or His) Lordship on the Bench, in the precincts of the Court, and whenever they are being approached in their judicial capacity.

In their private capacities they may be addressed in speech as 'Mr Justice Smith', as 'Judge', or as 'Sir John'.

In writing *Letter*

Formally According to circumstances: My Lord, *or*

Sir,

Socially Address by rank.

Envelope

The Hon. Mr Justice Swift (to a court address) *or*

The Hon. Sir John Swift (to a private address)

WOMEN   They are made Dame of the Most Excellent Order of the British Empire on their appointment.

In speech   Judges are addressed in Court as My Lady and Your (or Her) Ladyship. Socially they may be addressed as:

Mrs Justice . . . *or*

Dame . . .

The style 'Mrs Justice' was traditionally used by unmarried judges, but 'Ms Justice' is now used if preferred.

In writing   *Envelope*

The Hon. Dame . . . , DBE, *or*

The Hon. Mrs Justice . . . , DBE

As with **Circuit Judges** (*see* page 123), the second to be appointed of two High Court Judges with the same name will have chosen to be known by a forename in addition.

Queen's Counsel who are appointed High Court Judges no longer use the initials QC after their name.

Presidents of the Three High Court Divisions

The High Court has three divisions, Chancery, Queen's Bench, and Family Divisions.

The Lord Chief Justice of England is President of the Queen's Bench Division; the Chancellor of the High Court is head of the Chancery Division; and one of the judges of the Family Division is appointed its President.

These judges are not addressed as Hon. Mr Justice; the Lord Chief Justice is addressed as such (*see* page 132), and the other two by their names and offices, or by their offices alone.

In writing   *Envelope*

The Hon. Sir Charles Brown, The Chancellor *or*

The Chancellor

and

The Right Hon. Sir Maurice Smith, President of the Family Division *or*

The President of the Family Division

(Hon. or Right Hon. depending on whether the judge is a Privy Counsellor.)

Retired Judges of the High Court

After retirement, the address on the envelope is:

The Hon. Sir John Swift

Judges overseas

Judges of the High Courts or Supreme Courts of Commonwealth countries or overseas territories are addressed during office as:

The Honourable the Chief Justice, *or*

The Hon. Mr or Mrs Justice . . .

In Australia, Judges of the High Court are now addressed as The Hon. Justice . . .

The Chief Justice of Canada bears the title 'The Right Honourable' for life. Other Judges of Commonwealth countries may be Privy Counsellors, when they will be addressed as Right Hon. also. It is not unusual in some countries for a Judge who has held office for some time to be granted the title 'The Honourable' for life. Otherwise no special form of address is used on retirement.

Justices of the Peace

Justices of the Peace are also known as magistrates. They are volunteers who hear cases in courts in their community.

In speech	Justices of the Peace are addressed on the Bench as Your Worship.
In writing	*Envelope*
Formally	When writing to a Justice of the Peace in his or her official capacity (and only then), the affix JP should be used (*see* page 149).
Socially	As an **Esquire** (*see* page 65), or according to rank.

Justices of the Supreme Court of the United Kingdom

The Supreme Court of the United Kingdom was established in October 2009. The existing Law Lords became the first Justices of the Supreme Court; they continue to be Members of the House of Lord but are disqualified from sitting and voting until their retirement from the Supreme Court.

Justices appointed from October 2009 are not members of the House of Lords; though not necessarily Life Peers, they are styled 'Lord' and 'Lady' for life.

In speech	A Justice of the Supreme Court is addressed and referred to as My Lord *or* My Lady and His Lordship *or* Her Ladyship.
In writing	*Letter*
	They are addressed by professional, semi-professional and semi-official correspondents as:
	Dear Lord *or* Lady Smith,
In writing	*Envelope*
	The Right Hon. Lord *or* Lady Smith . . .
	or, privately,
	The Right Hon. Sir Henry . . .
	The Right Hon. Dame Elizabeth . . .

Lady Mayoresses

Rules as for wives of Lord Mayors apply (*see* page 133).

Law Lords

Formerly Lords of Appeal in Ordinary, when rules were as for **Life Peers** (*see* page 8), they are now known as Justices of the Supreme Court of the United Kingdom (*see* page 130).

Lord-Lieutenants and Lieutenants of Counties

Her Majesty's Lord-Lieutenants are the representatives of the Crown in each county in the United Kingdom.

In speech   Lord-Lieutenants are addressed according to their rank.

In writing   *Envelope*

His Grace the Duke of Middlesex, KG, HM Lord-Lieutenant for . . .

If a commoner, the form is:

Alan Smith, Esq., HM Lord-Lieutenant for . . . *or*

Mrs Angela Smith, HM Lord-Lieutenant for . . .

At the time of the amalgamation of some counties under the Local Government Act 1972, the appointment formerly known as HM Lieutenant (commonly called Lord-Lieutenant), became officially HM Lord-Lieutenant; and some additional appointments were made, so that a new county consisting of two or more formerly separate counties might have a Lord-Lieutenant and one or two Lieutenants. The appointment of a Lieutenant was only made when the new county included two counties each of which had previously had its own Lord-Lieutenant.

A Lieutenant is also addressed according to his or her rank, with the addition of the appointment:

Colonel J. S. Napier, DSO, HM Lieutenant for . . .

Lord Advocate of Scotland

The Lord Advocate is the senior Scottish Law Officer.

In speech

Formally and socially   Formerly addressed as My Lord, etc., but now, probably from ceasing to be on the Bench, more frequently as Sir. He or she is addressed socially as Lord Advocate.

He or she may be a member of the House of Lords or of the House of Commons, but need not be either; he or she is always a Privy Counsellor.

In writing   *Letter*

Dear Lord Advocate,

Envelope

The Right Hon. the Lord Advocate

Lord Chamberlain

The Lord Chamberlain is the senior officer of the Royal Household and is addressed according to rank and title.

Lord Chancellor

The Lord Chancellor is a senior member of the Cabinet and is addressed according to rank and title.

Prior to the Constitutional Reform Act of 2005 the Lord Chancellor was also Speaker of the House of Lords, head of the judiciary and the senior judge of the House of Lords.

Lord Chief Justice

The Lord Justice presides over the Queen's Bench Division of the High Court and is the head of the judiciary of England and Wales. If a life peer, as a member of the judiciary he is disqualified from sitting and voting in the House of Lords until his retirement.

In speech	The Lord Chief Justice is likely to be a peer, and is addressed and referred to accordingly.
In writing	*Letter*
Socially	A social letter may begin: Dear Lord Chief Justice,
Formally and socially	*Envelope* The Right Hon. the Lord Chief Justice of England

Lord Justice of Appeal

A Lord Justice of Appeal will already be a High Court Judge and therefore a knight or a dame. He or she will become a Privy Counsellor on appointment.

In speech	A Lord Justice of Appeal is addressed and referred to as My Lord or My Lady and His Lordship or Her Ladyship.
In writing	*Letter*
	They are addressed by professional, semi-professional and semi-official correspondents as:
	Dear Lord or Lady Justice,
In writing	*Envelope*
	The Right Hon. Lord or Lady Justice . . .
	or, privately,
	The Right Hon. Sir Henry . . .
	The Right Hon. Dame Elizabeth . . .

Lord of the Manor

Such a lordship confers no rank or title.

Lord Mayors

The Lord Mayors of Belfast, Cardiff, Dublin, London and York, and of the Australian cities of Adelaide, Brisbane, Hobart, Melbourne, Sydney, and Perth are entitled to the style Right Hon. while they are in office. This is, however, only an official and not a personal prefix, and it is used only with the title 'Lord Mayor' and not with the Lord Mayor's own name; it is incorrect to address such a Lord Mayor as, for example, 'The Right Hon. Richard Whittington'. The form of address does not vary when the Lord Mayor is a woman.

In speech	The formal mode of address is My Lord, while socially they are addressed according to their own name and rank.
In writing	*Letter*
	The formal mode of address is My Lord, while socially they are addressed according to their own name and rank.
	Envelope
	The Right Hon. the Lord Mayor of . . .

The Mayors of certain other cities also are designated 'Lord Mayors', and are addressed according to these rules, except as to the envelope which should be addressed:

The Right Worshipful the Lord Mayor of . . .

Lady Mayoresses (women)

The formal mode of address for a woman acting as Lady Mayoress (female consort of a Lord Mayor) is, both in speech and writing, My Lady. Lady Mayoresses do not share the honour of the style Right Hon. or Right Worshipful.

In writing	*Envelope*
	The Lady Mayoress of . . .

(men)

Where a man has the role of Lord Mayor's consort, it is best to ascertain his particular wishes. It is likely that he will wish to be addressed according to his own name and rank.

Lord Privy Seal

The Lord Privy Seal is a Great Officer of State and is addressed according to his or her own name and title.

Lord Provosts

Under the Local Government (Scotland) Act, 1973, the title of Lord Provost attaches to the Chairmen of the District Councils of Aberdeen, Dundee, Edinburgh and Glasgow.

The Lord Provost of Edinburgh and the Lord Provost of Glasgow should both be addressed as 'The Right Hon. the Lord Provost of . . . '; 'The Right Hon.' should not be used in front of their names. The form of address does not vary when the Lord Provost is a woman.

In speech	During office Lord Provosts are addressed and referred to as My Lord and His Lordship. The Lord Provost of Glasgow is referred to socially as 'The Lord Provost' and addressed as Lord Provost (not, except in historical comparison, Lord Provost Campbell).
In writing	*Letter*
	Dear Lord Provost,
	Envelope
	The Right Hon. the Lord Provost of Edinburgh (*or* Glasgow)
	The Lord Provost of . . .

Wives

Wives do not share the title, though there has been a tendency to refer to them as The Lady Provost, which has led to such incorrect descriptions as 'Lord Provost Campbell and the Lady Provost of . . . , which should be avoided.

Lords of Session

A Lord of Session is a Judge of the Court of Session (or Senator of the Court of Justice) of Scotland who, upon elevation to the Bench, is styled for life The Hon. Lord *or* Lady, with surname or a territorial name according to choice. This is a title of judicial office, and not a peerage.

If a Lord of Session is also a Privy Counsellor he or she is, or course, addressed as The Right Hon. Lord *or* Lady . . .

In speech   They are addressed as My Lord *or* My Lady.

In writing   *Letter*

Dear Lord . . . ,

Envelope

The Hon. Lord . . .

The Lord Justice-General and the Lord Justice-Clerk of Scotland are Lords of Session and Privy Counsellors. They are always addressed by their office:

The Right Hon. the Lord Justice-General

The Right Hon. the Lord Justice-Clerk

Upon giving up this office they revert to the style of a Lord of Session who is a Privy Counsellor.

Wives and Husbands

Wives are addressed in writing as Lady . . . , and in other respects as the wife of a Baron (*see* page 43), but without the prefix 'The Right Hon.' or 'The'. Husbands are addressed according to their own rank or office. Children have no title.

Magistrates

See under **Justices of the Peace** (page 129) and **District Judges (Magistrates' Courts)** (page 125).

Master of the Rolls

The Master of the Rolls is the Head of Civil Justice

Rules as for **Judges** apply (*see* page 127).

In writing   *Envelope*

The Right Hon. The Master of the Rolls *or*

The Right Hon. (according to rank)

Masters of the High Court

Masters of the High Court of England and Wales are judicial officers. They are addressed according to own name and rank, except in court, when they are addressed and referred to as, e.g. Master Robson.

Mayors

A Mayor is the highest-ranking officer in the municipal government of a town or city. The Mayors of certain cities use the description 'Lord Mayor' (*see* page 133 under that heading).

In speech   The formal mode of address for both men and women is 'Your Worship' or 'Mr Mayor', while socially they are addressed according to their own name and rank; colloquially 'Madam Mayor' is sometimes used, but this is not an established mode of address.

In writing   Mayors are addressed according to their own rank.

Envelope

Mayor of a city   The Right Worshipful the Mayor of . . .

Mayor of a   The Worshipful the Mayor of . . .
borough

Mayoresses and escorts

In speech   Mayoresses (female escorts of a Mayor) are addressed as 'Mayoress', never 'Your Worship', or 'Mr Mayor'. If a Mayoress is a Justice of the Peace and is sitting on the Bench, then the term 'Your Worship' would, of course, be used when addressing the Bench. Male escorts are addressed according to their own name and rank.

In writing   Mayoresses and escorts are addressed according to their own rank.

Directly Elected Mayors

Mayors in certain cities, towns and boroughs that have been directly elected by voters do not use the titles 'The Right Worshipful' or 'The Worshipful'. They are addressed according to their own rank or as 'The Mayor of . . . .'

The Mayor of London

The Mayor of London, not to be confused with the Lord Mayor of the City of London (see page 133), is elected alongside the London Assembly and first took office in 2000. No courtesy title has been given to the office of Mayor of London, who is to be addressed according to his own rank. Formally he is referred to as 'Mr Mayor' or 'The Mayor of London'.

Members of Parliament

Members of Parliament (House of Commons) are addressed according to rank, with MP after the name.

There is no established convention for the use of postnominals in the case of Members of the European Parliament, of the Scottish Parliament, of the National Assembly for Wales, of the Northern Ireland Assembly and of the House of Keys, Isle of Man.

Ministers (Government)

All cabinet ministers in the UK are Privy Counsellors and Members of Parliament (House of Commons or House of Lords). Otherwise they are addressed according to their own rank or title.

Ministers (Diplomatic Service)

In speech and writing	The title Envoy-Extraordinary and Minister-Plenipotentiary, given to the head of a Legation, was customarily abbreviated to Minister. Now all posts have been elevated to Ambassador, and all Legations to Embassy.

Ministers, Ministers (Economic), or Ministers (Commercial), may serve under the Ambassador in a large Embassy; but their title merely indicates their diplomatic service rank and they are not given any special form of address, as they would be if they were Ministers Plenipotentiary at the head of a Legation.

Police

For reasons of security, omit rank and occupation from any envelope sent to a home address.

Metropolitan and City of London Police

Commissioner, Deputy or Assistant Commissioner

Other Police Forces

Chief Constable, Deputy or Assistant Chief Constable

In speech	Men or women of these ranks are addressed by name or by appointment.

In writing	*Letter*
Formally	Dear Sir,
	Dear Madam,
Socially	Dear Mr (or Mrs, or Miss, or Ms) Dixon, *or*
	Dear Chief Constable
	Envelope
	The envelope is addressed with the name, followed by appointment and Force.
	Sir George Dixon, CBE
	Commissioner of the Metropolitan Police
	George Dixon, Esq., OBE
	Deputy Chief Constable, . . . Constabulary

Commanders, Chief Superintendents, Superintendents

In speech	Men or women of these ranks may be addressed either with the rank before the name or with Mr, Mrs, Miss or Ms.
In writing	*Letter*
	Same rules as above.
In writing	*Envelope*
	Superintendent G. D. Dixon
	. . . Constabulary
	G. D. Dixon, Esq., QPM
	Chief Superintendent, Metropolitan Police

Other Ranks

Below the ranks described above, the rank is always used before the name.

On envelopes the Force follows the name.

Presidents

Presidents of foreign countries should be addressed as Your Excellency and referred to as His/Her Excellency. The US president, however, should be addressed as Mr President and on envelopes as the President of the United States of America. Former US Presidents retain their title.

Prime Ministers

In the United Kingdom Prime Ministers are always Privy Counsellors and are so addressed, according to rank.

The Prime Ministers of many Commonwealth countries are also members of the Privy Council. If they are not Privy Counsellors, they are customarily addressed as Hon. during the period of office.

Provosts of Scottish Cities

A Provost is the ceremonial head of a local authority in Scotland.

Rules apply as in the case of an **Esquire** (*see* page 65) but a Provost will be referred to locally as The Provost, rather than 'Mr or Mrs . . . .'

The civic heads of Edinburgh, Dundee, Aberdeen, and Glasgow are known as Lord Provost (*see* page 134).

Queen's Counsel

A limited number of senior barristers 'take silk' by becoming Queen's Counsel. They should be addressed according to rank, with the initials QC appended to the name on envelopes.

When a Queen's Counsel is appointed a Circuit Judge, he or she continues to use the initials, but Judges of the High Court cease to use them.

Recorders

A Recorder is a part-time judge; they are barristers or solicitors. They should be addressed as an Esquire (*see* page 65), or according to rank.

On the bench they are addressed as 'Your Honour'.

The Recorders may be Queen's Counsel, in which case the initials QC should be added on envelopes.

Sheriffs

England, Wales and Northern Ireland

Sheriffs are appointed in all counties and in some cities, including the City of London, as officials of the Crown historically concerned with the administration of justice.

Sheriffs of counties are known as High Sheriffs, indicating that theirs is a senior appointment.

In speech	They may be addressed on formal occasions as High Sheriff (of counties), or Sheriff or Mr *or* Mrs Sheriff (of cities).
In writing	*Letter*
	The office of Sheriff requires no special form of address. Rules apply as in the case of an Esquire (*see* page 65), or according to rank.
In writing	*Envelope*
Official business	Colonel J. C. W. Browne, DSO High Sheriff of . . . shire

Scotland

Sheriffs are Judges of the Sheriff Courts. There are six Sheriffs-Principal, and within each of their jurisdictions a number of Sheriffs.

In speech

In court	My Lord *or* My Lady (whether Sheriff-Principal or Sheriff)
Officially and socially	Sheriff . . . (whether Sheriff-Principal or Sheriff)

The Sheriff-Principal is announced and referred to as the Sheriff-Principal of . . . (*see below, under envelope*).

In writing	*Letter*
	The office requires no special form of address. Rules apply as in the case of an **Esquire** (*see* page 65), or according to rank.
	Envelope
	Rules apply as follows:

Part-time:	Esq. (or according to rank)
Full-time:	Sheriff Robert Mackenzie

The Sheriff-Principal is, however, addressed as:

William Douglas, Esq. (or according to rank)
        Sheriff-Principal of . . .

using the first territorial name of conjoined shrievalties (areas of jurisdiction).

Tribunal Judges

Tribunal Judges can be legally-qualified or non-legal appointments and they are assigned to a particular specialist area. They are addressed according to name and rank.

Vice Lord-Lieutenants

Vice Lord-Lieutenants are appointed from among the Deputy Lieutenants to support the Lord-Lieutenant.

They are addressed according to name and rank. The abbreviation VL following the name is not used.

THE UNIVERSITIES

Chancellors

The Chancellor is the ceremonial head of a university.

In speech	Chancellors are addressed formally as Sir *or* Madam, or according to rank. More familiarly as Mr Chancellor or Chancellor.
In writing	*Letter*
Formally	Sir *or* Madam (or according to rank),
	I am, Sir *or* Madam,
	Your obedient servant,
Less formally	Dear Sir *or* Madam,
	Yours faithfully,
Socially	Dear Chancellor,
	Yours sincerely,
	Envelope
	John Mansfield, Esq.
	Chancellor of the University of . . . *or*
	The Right Hon. the Earl of . . .
	Chancellor of the University of . . .

Vice-Chancellors

The Vice-Chancellor is the executive head of a university and may carry the title President and Vice-Chancellor.

In speech	The rules as for Chancellors apply. The prefix is used only with the office, not with the individual's name.
In writing	*Letter*
Formally	The rules as for Chancellors apply.
Socially	Dear Vice-Chancellor,
	Yours sincerely,
	Envelope
	The Vice-Chancellor of The University of . . .

The two exceptions to this are Vice-Chancellors of Oxford and Cambridge, who are addressed respectively as:

The Rev. the Vice-Chancellor of The University of Oxford (whether or not the Vice-Chancellor is in Holy Orders) *and*

The Right Worshipful the Vice-Chancellor of The University of Cambridge

High Stewards

High Stewards are officials appointed in the Universities of Oxford and Cambridge.

In speech	They are addressed according to their rank.
In writing	*Letter*
Formally	Sir (or according to rank),
	I am, Sir,
	Your obedient servant,
Less formally	Dear Sir,
	Yours faithfully,
Socially	Dear High Steward,
	Yours sincerely,
	Envelope
	His Grace the Duke of . . .
	High Steward of The University of . . .

Deputy High Stewards

Rules apply as for **High Stewards**.

Heads of Colleges

They may be known as Masters, Mistresses, Presidents, Principals, Provosts, Rectors, or Wardens.

In speech	They are addressed formally as Sir or Madam.
	Socially by name and rank.

In writing	*Letter*
Formally	Sir *or* Madam (or according to rank),
	Your obedient servant,
Less formally	Dear Sir *or* Madam (or according to rank),
	Yours faithfully,
Socially	Dear Master *or* Mistress (or according to college title),
	Yours sincerely,
	Envelope
	The Master (or according to college title) of . . . College

Deans

Deans of colleges are addressed according to their own name and rank. In the rare cases (cathedral colleges) where a dean is head he will also be a dean of the Church of England and must be addressed as such (*see* page 80).

Principals in Scotland and Wales

The head of a Scottish or Welsh University may carry the title Principal and Vice-Chancellor.

The same rules of address apply as for **Vice-Chancellors** (*see* page 142).

Professors

In speech	The title is used both formally and socially.
In writing	*Letter*
Formally	Dear Sir (*or* Madam),
	I am, dear Sir (*or* Madam),
	Your obedient servant,
Less formally	Dear Sir (*or* Madam),
	Yours faithfully,
Socially	Dear Professor Dash,
	Yours sincerely,
	Envelope
	Professor J. G. Dash

Ordained Professors

In speech   An ordained professor is referred and spoken to as a Professor.

In writing   *Letter*

As for a Professor.

Envelope

The Rev. Professor W. L. Fleetwood

If Canon, he or she is addressed as such (*see* page 82). Such accumulations as Professor the Rev. Canon . . . , though not unknown, are undesirable.

Doctors

Degrees are given by the older and most of the newer universities in seven faculties: Divinity, Law, Literature, Medicine, Music, Philosophy and Science. The following are the various styles and abbreviations:

Doctor of Divinity   DD

Doctor of Laws   LLD

Conferred by Cambridge and all other universities granting degrees in this faculty.

Doctor of Civil Law   DCL

This is the Oxford, Durham and Newcastle upon Tyne degree corresponding to the Cambridge LLD.

Doctor of Literature/	LittD	Cambridge, Dublin and Liverpool
Doctor of Letters	DLitt	Oxford and some others
	DLit	London and Manchester
Doctor of Medicine	MD	all universities except Oxford
	DM	Oxford
Doctor of Music	MusD	Cambridge and Durham
	DMus	Oxford
Doctor of Philosophy	PhD	Cambridge and others
	DPhil	Oxford
Doctor of Science	ScD	Cambridge and Dublin
	DSc	Oxford and others

In writing	*Letter*
	Rules as for Esquires, with Dr substituted for Mr, Mrs or Miss.

Envelope

It is a matter of individual choice whether the holder of a doctorate is addressed as Dr . . . or as John . . . , Esq., with the appropriate lettering, except that it is now the custom always to write the letters DD (*See also* **Doctors of Medicine**, *below*).

It is never correct to write Dr . . . , PhD (or whatever the lettering may be).

Outside academic circles even doctorates would not be appended to the name in social letters, although of course, anyone customarily known as Dr . . . would still be so.

Doctors of Divinity

Doctors of Divinity are usually but not always clergymen. The degree can, in some universities, be taken by, or conferred on, laymen as well.

In speech	They are addressed and referred to as Dr Read, even in the case of the clergy.

In writing	*Letter*
Formally	Reverend Sir,
	Yours faithfully,
Socially	Dear Dr Read,
	Yours sincerely,
	Envelope
	The Rev. J. L. Read, DD

Doctors of Medicine

The title has become so wedded to the medical profession that the reminder is needed that not all qualified medical men hold the final degree.

Those who hold the final degree are addressed and referred to as Dr Gray. Those medical men who have not taken the final degree are addressed as if they have. There is also the firmly established custom in the medical profession of addressing surgeons as Esquires.

Gynaecologists tend to be addressed as surgeons in England and Wales, as doctors elsewhere.

If a knighthood, baronetcy or peerage has been conferred, the address is according to rank.

In speech   Specialists and general practitioners are addressed as Dr, surgeons as Mr, Mrs or Miss unless the doctor has a rank above Esquire in which case rules for the particular rank will apply.

In writing   *Letter*

According to rank. It is normal, however, to address general practitioners as Dr.

Envelope

Fully qualified doctors:

Thomas Gray, Esq., MD (but in Scotland, usually, Dr Thomas Gray)

Sir Thomas Gray, MD

Sir Thomas Gray, Bt, MD

The Right Hon. Lord Gray, MD

Doctors without final degrees take the letters relating to their qualification, e.g. MB, LRCP. It is normal to address general practitioners simply as Dr Thomas Gray, without letters.

Surgeons:

Thomas Gray, Esq., FRCS *etc.*

Honorary Doctorates

The same rules apply as to other holders, although it is not usual to add letters after the name if there are other letters already. They may appear in the most comprehensive lists but they are not used in circumstances where they may seem to imply an academic qualification.

Lesser Degrees

The custom established and used by the older universities is really the best to follow. The rule is that doctors in any faculty use the designation (see **Doctors**), while lesser degrees are omitted.

Letters denoting masters' and bachelors' degrees, which are, of course, most common, are not used even in university circles in ordinary correspondence, and socially they are not used at all. There are certain formal occasions on which members of learned professions would use them, such as in lists of lectures, etc., but a master's or bachelor's degree would not be appended to a doctor's. The reason for this is that in the older universities a doctor's degree is considered to include an MA – it can only very rarely be taken without it.

Only the higher of two degrees in the same faculty would be used.

Master of Arts	MA
Bachelor of Arts	BA
Bachelor of Letters	BLitt
Bachelor of Divinity	BD
Master of Laws	LLM
Bachelor of Laws	LLB
Bachelor of Civil Law	BCL
Bachelor of Medicine	MB
Bachelor of Medicine	BM (Oxford)
Bachelor of Music	BMus
	MusB
	MusBac
Bachelor of Science	BSc

HONOURS, QUALIFICATIONS AND APPOINTMENTS

Notes on the Use of Abbreviations for Honorific and Other Affixes

Honorific affixes, whether military decorations or not, should be appended in addressing formal letters; but not in the case of Privy Counsellors.

Affixes indicating professional qualification or official status should be used only when addressing the correspondent in his or her professional or official capacity. This includes DL and JP.

> To some extent it is a matter of personal preference how many letters are used after the name. For modesty or simplicity, someone might use only the most distinguished medical qualifications or professional fellowships.

The order of letters after the name (and after the abbreviations Bt or Esq., if they apply) is fixed, and should be followed as set out below.

First **Decorations and Honours**

These should not be omitted, if any letters are used at all, and in most cases it is preferable to include them in an address. They should be written in the sequence given on page 151.

Second **Appointments made by or on behalf of the Queen**

If for any reason it is necessary to include the initials PC, they will come first, followed by ADC, QHP, QHS, QHDS, QHC, QC, JP, DL. It should be noted, however, that PC is nowadays never used on envelopes, and that the next appointments (up to QHC) being short-term ones, are not normally used in ordinary correspondence, although they may be in official letters.

QC must always be used. JP and DL are used when writing on business connected with the appointment.

Third **University Degrees**

See pages 145–147.

Fourth

Medical Qualifications Other than University Degrees

In normal correspondence only those indicating fellowships or memberships are used. Medical precede surgical and are followed by more specialised fellowships. FRCP and FRCS should always appear (in that order) if held, and so should fellowships or memberships of other institutions that confer postgraduate qualifications.

Fifth

Fellowships or Memberships of Learned Societies, Academies or Professional Institutions

As a general rule, letters should be shown in the order of the foundation of the societies, etc., and no distinction is made, in the sequence, between fellowships and memberships. Where, however, a professional institution has fellows and members, only letters for the higher rank would be shown on any but professional correspondence.

Those fellowships, etc., election to which is a distinction should be used on all correspondence: FRS, RA or FRA, RSA, FBA are examples.

Initials which indicate merely that the fellow or member declares his interest in and support for the body concerned are used when the subject of his or her interest is the matter of the correspondence.

Initials are also used to indicate professional eminence or qualification when writing on professional matters.

The members of the sixteen bodies which make up the institutions of the Engineering Council are chartered engineers; they are entitled to use the letters CEng, which are placed immediately before the first fellowship or membership that gives the right to use such initials:

J. B. MacTavish, Esq., CEng, MICE, FIMechE.

Similarly, fellows and members of the Royal Society of Chemistry are entitled to use the abbreviation CChem before the letters FRSC and MRSC.

Sixth

Appointments or Offices

These include such initials as MP, MLA, MLC, WS.

Sequence of Decorations and Honours

The following list shows the correct sequence of the various degrees of Honours and Decorations of which the abbreviations are most commonly employed. A higher rank in an Order includes the lower, i.e. it is never correct to put GCB, KCB, or KCMG, CMG. All decorations and honours should be given.

For the sequence of letters after the name other than decorations and honours, *see* pages 149–150.

For the various orders of Knighthood, *see* pages 52–59.

For the explanation of abbreviations, *see* preliminary pages of this book.

VC, GC, KG/LG, KT/LT, GCB, OM, GCMG, GCVO, GBE, CH, KCB/DCB, KCMG/DCMG, KCVO/DCVO, KBE/DBE, CB, CMG, CVO, CBE, DSO, LVO, OBE, ISO, MVO, MBE, RRC, DSC, MC, DFC, AFC, ARRC, AM, DCM, CGM, GM, DSM, MM, DFM, AFM, QGM, BEM, QPM, SGM, VD, ERD, TD, ED, RD, VRD, AE.

Victoria Cross

The Victoria Cross is the most distinguished of all decorations, and is conferred for valour in all branches of the fighting services. Created in 1856 by Queen Victoria, since 1920 it has been extended to include women. The abbreviation VC takes precedence of all other decorations and honours.

Other service decorations may be used in accordance with the list above in addressing a recipient in writing.

George Cross

The George Cross was created in 1940 by George VI and is awarded for acts of great heroism or of conspicuous courage in extreme danger. It is intended primarily for civilians (both men and women), but awards are also made to members of the fighting services in actions for which military honours are not normally granted. The abbreviation GC follows VC but takes precedence of all other decorations and honours.

Order of Merit – OM

The Order of Merit was created in 1902 by Edward VII to recognise nationally distinguished contributions in science, art, music, literature and public life. It is a very distinguished order, limited to twenty-four members, ranking in precedence immediately after Knights Grand Cross of the Order of the Bath.

Order of the Companions of Honour – CH

The Order of the Companions of Honour was created in 1917 and is awarded to people who perform important service to the nation in select fields. The order is limited to sixty-five members, for which women are equally eligible with men. It carries no titles, but holders use the initials CH after the name. It ranks in precedence after the 1st degree of the Order of the British Empire (GBE).

Commonwealth Countries

Many Commonwealth countries have instituted their own orders which are awarded to their own citizens and which are indicated (in the British fashion) by postnominal lettering.

Such orders may be conferred on citizens of other countries within the Commonwealth who have in some way served the country awarding the honour. It is customary to use the letters or distinguishing titles of such orders while in the country that conferred them, but not elsewhere.

For awards in all Commonwealth countries, information can be obtained from the office of the Governor General or equivalent head of state.

Antigua and Barbuda

Knight of the Most Exalted Order of the National Hero – KNH

The Most Distinguished Order of the Nation has three classes:

Knight Grand Collar – KGN

Knight Grand Cross – KGCN

Knight (or Dame) Commander – KCN/DCN

Australia

The Order of Australia has four grades:

Knight (or Dame) of the Order of Australia – AK, AD

> #### Knight (or Dame) of the Order of Australia
> This grade, established in 1976, was disestablished in 1986 on the advice of Prime Minister Bob Hawke. It was reinstated on the advice of Prime Minister Tony Abbott in 2014 but again disestablished on the advice of Prime Minister Bill Shorten in 2015.

Companion of the Order of Australia – AC

Officer of the Order of Australia – AO

Member of the Order of Australia – AM

These letters follow respectively OM, GBE, KBE and DSO.

Barbados

The Order of Barbados has four classes:

Knight (or Dame) of St Andrew – KA, DA whose letters follow CH

Companion of Honour of Barbados – CHB

The Crown of Merit, which is in two grades:

>The Gold Crown of Merit – GCM

>The Silver Crown of Merit – SCM

The Barbados Service Award, which is in two grades:

>The Barbados Service Star – BSS

>The Barbados Service Medal – BSM

Canada

The Order of Canada confers three honours:

Companion of the Order of Canada – CC

Officer of the Order of Canada – OC

Member of the Order of Canada – CM

The Order of Military Merit has three grades:

Commander of the Order – CMM

Officer of the Order – OMM

Member of the Order – MMM

VC or GC would precede any of these letters.

Following letters for the Order of Canada and the Order of Military Merit come letters for Canadian provincial orders:

Ordre national du Québec – GOQ, OQ, CQ

The Saskatchewan Order of Merit – SOM

The Order of Ontario – OOnt

The Order of British Columbia – OBC

Alberta Order of Excellence – AOE

Jamaica

The Order of Jamaica (member) – OJ

Letters entitle bearer to title 'Hon.'

New Zealand

The Order of New Zealand (member) – ONZ whose letters follow OM

The New Zealand Order of Merit has five grades whose letters follow ONZ:

Knight (or Dame) Grand Companion – GNZM

Knight (or Dame) – KNZM, DNZM

Companion – CNZM

Officer – ONZM

Member – MNZM

The Queen's Service Order of New Zealand – the letters QSO precede OBE, and QSM (Queen's Service Medal) follow QGM.

REPLYING FORMALLY TO FORMAL INVITATIONS

Royal invitations from the Queen

Invitations are sent by a member of the Queen's household:

	The Lord Chamberlain
or	The Lord Steward of the Household
or	The Master of the Household

and replies should be addressed to the official who has sent the invitation.

Those who have received the invitation should reply formally, giving their name in the same form that appears on the invitation itself, *viz*

Mr and Mrs Albert Green

Hon. and Mrs Albert Green

Rev. and Mrs Albert Green

Hence:	Mr and Mrs Albert Green present their compliments to the Lord Chamberlain,
or	the Lord Steward of the Household,
or	the Master of the Household,

and then, either: and have the honour to obey Her Majesty's Command to

e.g.	the state banquet on 9 November at 8 p.m.
	the garden party on 14 June at 3 p.m.
	luncheon on 23 March at 1 p.m.
or	and much regret that they will be unable to obey Her Majesty's Command to . . . on . . . , owing to the illness of Mrs Albert Green. (The reason should be specific and adequate – a minor engagement would not be considered sufficient reason not to obey the Command.)

Royal invitations from other members of the Royal Family

The procedures follow a similar pattern, but the invitations are no longer commands, so the reply should be worded

Mr and Mrs Albert Green present their compliments to (the person who has sent the invitation)

and have much pleasure in accepting the invitation from (e.g.) HRH The Prince of Wales to the luncheon on 23 March at 1 p.m.

or   . . . and much regret that they are unable to accept the invitation from His Royal Highness owing to . . .

Invitations to official functions

Invitations are often accompanied by a printed reply card. This should always be used and rules out the need for other reply.

Where there is no such card, write a letter (with the address at the head):

Mr and Mrs Albert Green thank (e.g.) the Chairman and Council of the National Association of . . . for their kind invitation for Friday, 15 October, which they accept with much pleasure.

or   . . . which they much regret being unable to accept.

(Here, another engagement could be adequate reason if a reason is given.)

Invitations to private functions (including weddings)

Invitations are frequently addressed to, say, Mr/Mrs/Miss Evelyn Jones *and partner*, or *and family*. In a reply accepting the invitation, the names of those who will attend should be given.

Write a letter (with the address at the head) similar to that for official functions, but it should be written (and the envelope addressed) to the hostess only, even where the invitation comes from host and hostess.

In the case of weddings and similar social functions, there is an increasing tendency to reply informally, in which case the above recommendations do not apply.

Some Pronunciations of Proper Names

a	as in cat	ō	as in home
ah	as in father	o	as in dog
ay	as in day	ōō	as in food
g	as in good	oo	as in hood
i	as in pin	ow	as in how
		y	as in spy

A

Abergavenny	Aber-ga-*ven*-i (town), Aber-*gen*-i (title)
Abinger	*Ab*-binjer
Acheson	*Ach*-ison
Achonry	*Acon*-ri
Ackroyd	*Ak*-roid
Agate	*Ay*-gat
Ailesbury	*Ayls*-bri
Ailsa	*Ayl*-sa
Aitchison	*Aych*-ison
Akerman	*Ack*-erman
Akers-Douglas	*Ay*-kers-*Dug*-glas
Alcester	*Aw*-ster
Aldenham	*Awl*-dnam
Alington	*Al*-ington
Alleyne	*Al*-leen, Al-*lane*, *Al*-len
Allhusen	Al-*hew*-sen
Alnemouth	*Ayl*-mouth
Alnwick	*An*-nick
Alresford	*Awl*-sford
Althorp	*Awl*-thorp (formerly *Awl*-trup)
Altrincham	*Awl*-tringam
Amory	*A*-mori
Ampthill	*Amt*-hill
Annaly	*An*-nali
Annesley	*An*-sli
Anstruther	*An*-struther
Antrobus	*An*-trobus

Arbuthnott	Ar-*buth*-not
Archdall	*Arch*-dale
Ardagh	*Ar*-da
Ardee	Ar-*dee*
Argyll	Ar-*gyle*
Armagh	Ar-*mah*
Ashburnham	*Ash*-burnam
Ashburton	*Ash*-burton
Ashcombe	*Ash*-com
Assheton	*Ash*-ton
Atherton	*Ath*-erton
Athlumney	Ath-*lum*-ni
Atholl	*Ath*-ol
Auchinleck	*Aff*-leck, *Awk*-inleck
Auchterlonie	*Aukh*-ter-*lōn*-i
Ava	*Ah*-va
Ayers	Airs

B

Baden-Powell	*Bay*-dn-*Pō*-ell
Bagehot	*Baj*-jut
Baggallay	*Bag*-gali
Balcarres	Bal-*car*-riss
Baldry	*Bawl*-dri
Balfour	*Bal*-four
Balgonie	Bal-*gōn*-i
Balogh	Ballog
Bamfyld	*Bam*-feeld
Barham	*Bah*-ram
Barnardiston	Barnar-*dis*-ton
Barraclough	*Bar*-racluff
Barttelot	*Bart*-ilot
Barwick	*Bar*-rick, also as spelt
Bateson	*Bayt*-son
Battye	*Bat*-ti
Baugh	Baw
Beaconsfield	*Beck*-onsfield (town), *Bee*-consfield (title)

Beatty	*Bee*-ti
Beauchamp	*Bee*-cham
Beauclerc/k	*Bō*-clare
Beaufort	*Bō*-fort
Beaulieu	*Bew*-li
Beaumont	*Bō*-mont
Belisha	Be-*lee*-sha
Bellamy	*Bel*-lami
Bellew	*Bell*-yew, Bell-*ōō*
Bellingham	*Bell*-injam, *Bell*-ingam
Belvoir	*Bee*-ver
Berkeley	*Bark*-li
Berkshire	*Bark*-shere
Berners	*Ber*-ners
Bertie	*Bar*-ti
Besley	*Beez*-li, *Bez*-li
Bessborough	*Bez*-burra
Bethune	*Bee*-ton
Bicester	*Bis*-ter
Biddulph	*Bid*-dulf
Bigelow	*Big*-gelō
Bispham	*Bis*-pam
Blakiston	*Black*-iston
Blois	Bloyce
Blomefield, Blomfield	*Blōōm*-field
Blount	Blunt
Blyth	Bly, Blyth
Bois	Boyce
Boleyn	*Boo*-len, *Bo*-linn, *Bull*-in
Bolingbroke	*Bol*-linbrook
Bolitho	By-*ly*-thō
Bompas	*Bum*-pas
Bonsor	*Bon*-sor
Boord	Bord
Borrowes	*Bur*-rōze
Borthwick	*Borth*-wick
Bosanquet	*Bōzn*-ket
Boscawen	Bo-*scō*-en, Bo-*scaw*-en

Bosham	*Boz*-um
Boughey	*Bow*-i
Boughton	*Bow*-ton, *Baw*-ton
Bourchier	*Bow*-cher
Bourke	Berk
Bourne	Born, Bern, Bourn
Bowles	Bōlz
Brabazon	*Brab*-bazon
Brabourne	*Bray*-bn
Breadalbane	Bred-*awl*-ban
Brechin	*Breek*-hin
Broke	Brook
Brough	Bruff
Brougham	Brōōm
Broughton	*Braw*-ton
Buccleuch	Buck-*lōō*
Buchan	*Buk*-han
Buchanan	Bu-*can*-non, Bew-*can*-non
Burbury	*Ber*-bery
Burges	*Ber*-jez
Burghclere	*Ber*-clair
Burghersh	*Ber*-gersh
Burghley	*Ber*-li
Burroughes	*Bur*-rōz
Bury	*Ber*-ri, *Bew*-ri

C

Caccia	Katcha
Cadogan	Ka-*dug*-gan
Cahill	*Kay*-hill
Caillard	*Ky*-ar
Caius	Kees
Calderon	*Kawld*-eron
Callaghan	*Kall*-ahan, *Kall*-igan
Calthorpe	*Kawl*-thorp
Camoys	Kam-*oys*
Campden	*Kam*-den

Capell	*Kay*-pel
Carbery	*Kar*-beri
Carew	*Kair*-i, Ka-*rōō*
Carlyon	Kar-*ly*-on
Carmichael	Kar-*my*-kal
Carnegie	Kar-*neg*-gi
Carnwath	*Karn*-woth
Carpmael	*Karp*-male
Carruthers	Kar-*ruth*-ers
Carshalton	Kar-*shaw*-ton
Cassilis	*Kas*-sels
Castlereagh	*Kah*-selray
Cavan	*Kav*-van
Cavanagh	*Kav*-vana
Chalmers	*Chah*-mers
Chaloner	*Chal*-loner
Chandos	*Shan*-dos
Charlemont	*Shar*-le-mont
Charteris	*Char*-teris, *Char*-ters
Cheetham	*Cheet*-am
Cherwell	*Char*-well
Chetwode	*Chet*-wood
Chetwynd	*Chet*-wind
Cheylesmore	*Chil*-smor
Cheyne	Chain, *Chay*-ni, Cheen
Chichele	*Chich*-eli, Chi-*chai*-ley
Chisholm	*Chiz*-zom
Chiswick	*Chiz*-ik
Cholmeley, Cholmondeley, Chomley	*Chum*-li
Cirencester	*Syr*-ensester
Clanricarde	Klan-*rick*-ard
Clarina	Kla-*reen*-a
Claverhouse	*Klay*-vers, also as spelt
Clerk	Klark
Clerke	Klark
Cliveden	*Kliv*-den

Clogher	*Klo*-her
Cloncurry	Klun-*cur*-ri
Clonmell	Klon-*mel*
Clough	Kluff
Clowes	Klews, Klows
Clwyd	*Klew*-id
Cochrane	*Kock*-ran
Cockburn	*Kō*-burn
Coghill	*Kog*-hill
Coke	Kook, Kōk
Colborne	*Kole*-burn
Colles	*Kol*-lis
Colquhoun	Ko-*hōōn*
Colville	*Koll*-vil, *Kōl*-vil
Combe	Kōōm
Compton	*Kump*-ton, *Komp*-ton
Conisborough	*Kun*-sbra, *Kon*-is-bura
Constable	*Kun*-stable
Conyngham	*Kun*-ningam
Copleston	*Kop*-pelston
Corcoran	*Kork*-ran
Cottenham	*Kot*-tenam
Cottesloe	*Kot*-slō
Couch	Kōōch
Courtenay, Courtney	*Kort*-ni
Courthope	*Kort*-ōpe
Courtown	*Kor*-town
Cousens	*Kuz*-zens
Coutts	Kōōts
Coventry	*Kov*-entri, *Kuv*-entri
Coverdale	*Kuv*-erdale
Coverley	*Kuv*-erli
Cowell	*Kow*-ell, *Kō*-ell
Cowen	*Kō*-en, *Kow*en
Cowles	Kōlz
Cowper	*Kōō*-per, *Kow*-per
Cozens	*Kuz*-zens
Craigavon	Craig-*a*-von

Craster	*Crah*-ster
Crawshay	*Kraw*-shay
Creagh	Kray
Creighton	*Kry*-ton
Crespigny	*Krep*-ni
Crichton	*Kry*-ton
Croghan	*Krō*-an
Cromartie	*Krum*-marti
Crombie	*Krum*-bi
Culme-Seymour	*Kulm-See*-mer
Cuningham, Cuninghame, Cunyngham	*Kun*-ningam

D

Dacre	*Day*-ker
Dacres	*Day*-kers
Dahrendorf	*Darr*-endorf
Dalbiac	*Dawl*-biac
Dalgleish	Dal-*gleesh*
Dalhousie	Dal-*how*-zi
Dalmeny	Dal-*men*-ni
Dalrymple	Dal-*rim*-ple
Dalziel	Dee-*ell,* Dal-*zeel*
Daubeney	*Daw*-bni
Daventry	As spelt
Death	De-*ath*
De Burgh	De *Berg*
Decies	*Dee*-shees
De Crespigny	De *Krep*-ni
De Hoghton	De *Hor*-ton
De la Poer	De la *Poor*
De la Warr	*De*-laware
De l'Isle	De *Lyle*
De Moleyns	*Dem*-moleens
De Montmorency	De Montmor-*en*-si
Denbigh	*Den*-bi

Derby	*Dar*-bi
Dering	*Deer*-ing
De Rohan	De *Ro*-an
De Ros	De *Rōōs*
Derwent	*Dar*-went, also as spelt
De Salis	De *Sal*-lis, De Sahls
De Saumarez,	De *So*-marez
De Sausmarez	
Devereux	*Dev*-verōō, *Dev*-verōōx
De Vesci	De *Vess*-i
D'Eyncourt	*Dain*-curt
De Zoete	De *Zōōt*
Dillwyn	*Dil*-lon
Disraeli	Diz-*rail*-i
Donegal	*Don*-igawl
Doneraile	*Dun*-erayl
Donoghue	*Dun*-nohōō
Donoughmore	*Dun*-nomor
Dougall	*Dōō*-gal
Doughty	*Dow*-ti
Douglas	*Dug*-las
Drogheda	*Draw*-eda
Du Cane	Dew *Kane*
Duchesne	Du-*kahn*
Ducie	*Dew*-ssi
Dumaresq	Doo-*mer*-rick
Dumfries	Dum-*freess*
Dunalley	Dun-*nal*-li
Dundas	Dun-*das*
Dungarvan	Dun-*gar*-van
Dunglass	Dun-*glass*
Dunmore	Dun-*mor*
Dunsany	Dun-*sa*-ni
Duntze	Dunts
Dupplin	*Dup*-plin
Du Quesne	Dew *Kane*
Durand	Dew-*rand*
Durrant	Dur-*rant*, *Dur*-rant

Dwyfor	*Dwy*-for
Dymoke	*Dim*-muk
Dynevor	*Din*-nevor
Dysart	*Dy*-sart

E

Eardley-Wilmot	*Erd*-li-*Wil*-mot
Ebrington	*Ebb*-rington
Ebury	*Ee*-beri
Edgcumbe	*Ej*-cum, *Edg*-cum
Edwardes	*Ed*-wards
Egerton	*Ej*-erton, *Edg*-erton
Elam	*Ee*-lam
Elcho	*El*-kō
Elibank	*El*-libank
Eliot	*Ell*-iot
Ellesmere	*Els*-meer
Elphinstone	*El*-finston
Elwes	El-*weez*
Enniskillen	*In*-nis-*kil*-len
Ernle	*Ern*-li
Esmonde	*Ez*-mond
Etheredge	*Eth*-erij
Evershed	*Ev*-ershed
Ewart	*U*-art
Eyre	Air
Eyton	*Y*-ton

F

Falconbridge	*Fawk*-onbrij
Falconer	*Fawk*-ner
Falkland	*Fawk*-land
Farquhar	*Fark*-wer, *Fark*-er
Farquharson	*Fark*-werson, *Fark*-erson
Fawcett	*Faw*-set, *Foss*-et
Featherstonhaugh	*Feth*-erstonhaw

Feilden	*Feel*-den
Feilding	*Feel*-ding
Fenwick	*Fen*-ick
Fermanagh	*Fer*-mana
Feversham	*Fav*-ersham
Ffolkes	Fōks
Ffoulkes	Fōks, Fōōks
Fiennes	Fynes
Findlater	*Fin*-litter
Findlay	*Fin*-li
Fingall	*Fin*-gawl
Fitzhardinge	Fitz-*hard*-ing
Fleming	*Flem*-ming
Foljambe	*Fool*-jam
Forbes	Forbs
Fortescue	*Fort*-iskew
Foulis	Fowls
Fowey	Foy
Fowke	Fōk
Freake	Freek
Fremantle	Free-*man*-tle
Freyer	*Free*-ar, *Fry*-er
Froude	Frōōd
Furneaux	*Fur*-nō

G

Gairdner	*Gard*-ner
Galbraith	Gal-*brayth*
Gallagher	*Gal*-laher
Gallwey, Galway	*Gawl*-way
Garmoyle	Gar-*moyl*
Garnock	*Gar*-nock
Garvagh	*Gar*-va
Gatacre	*Gat*-taker
Gathorne	*Gay*-thorn
Geddes	*Ged*-diz, *Ged*-dess
Gee	Gee, Jee

Geikie	*Gee*-ki
Gell	Gell, Jell
Geoghegan	*Gay*-gun
Gerard	*Jer*-rard
Gervis-Meyrick	*Jer*-vis-*Mer*-ick
Gethen, Gethin, Gething	*Geth*-in, *Geeth*-in
Gibbes	Gibbs
Giddens	*Gid*-dens
Giffard	*Gif*-fard, *Jif*-fard
Gilhooly	Gil-*hōō*-li
Gilkes	Jilks
Gill	Gill, Jill
Gilles	*Gill*-is
Gillespie	Gill-*ess*-pi
Gillingham	*Jill*-ingam (Kent), *Gill*-ingam (Dorset)
Gilmour	*Gil*-mor
Gilroy	*Gil*-roy
Glamis	Glahms
Glerawly	Gler-*aw*-li
Goldsworthy	*Gōls*-worthi
Gomme	Gom
Gorges	*Gor*-jiz
Gormanston	*Gor*-manston
Goschen	*Gō*-shen
Gough	Goff
Goulburn	*Gōōl*-burn
Gourley	*Gor*-li
Gower	Gaw, also as spelt
Graeme	Gram, *Gray*-am
Grahame	*Gray*-am
Granard	*Gran*-nard
Greaves	Graves, Greeves
Greenhalgh	*Green*-how, *Green*-haltch
Greig	Greg
Greville	*Grev*-el
Grier	Greer
Grosvenor	*Grōv*-nor
Guildford	*Gil*-ford

Guinness	*Gin*-iss
Gwatkin	*Gwot*-kin
Gwynedd	*Gwin*-eth
Gye	Jy

H

Haden	*Hay*-dn
Haggard	*Hag*-gard
Haigh	Hayg
Haldane	*Hawl*-dane
Haldon	*Hawl*-don
Hallé	*Hal*-lay
Halsbury	*Hawl*-sbri
Halsey	*Hawl*-si, *Hal*-si
Hamond	*Ham*-mond
Hampden	*Ham*-den
Hanbury	*Han*-buri
Harberton	*Har*-berton
Harcourt	*Har*-curt, *Har*-cort
Hardinge	*Har*-ding
Harewood	*Har*-wood
Harington	*Ha*-rington
Harlech	*Har*-lick
Hawarden	*Hay*-warden, *Har*-den
Headlam	*Hed*-lam
Heathcote	*Heth*-cot
Hegarty	*Heg*-arti
Heneage	*Hen*-ij
Hennessey, Hennessy	*Hen*-essi
Henniker	*Hen*-iker
Henriques	Hen-*reek*-iz
Hepburn	*Heb*-burn
Herries	*Her*-ris
Herschell	*Her*-shel
Hertford	*Har*-ford
Hervey	*Her*-vi, *Har*-vi
Heytesbury	*Hayt*-sburi

Hindlip	*Hind*-lip
Hobart	*Hō*-bart, *Hub*-bart
Holbech	*Hol*-beech
Holmes	Hōmz
Holmesdale	*Hōmz*-dale
Holm-Patrick	Hōm-Patrick
Home	Hume, also as spelt
Honyman	*Hun*-niman
Honywood	*Hun*-niwood
Hopetoun	*Hope*-ton
Hotham	*Huth*-am
Hough	Huff
Houghton	*Huf*-ton, *Haw*-ton, *How*-ton, *Hō*-ton
Houston	*Hoost*-on
Howorth	*How*-erth
Hugessen	*Hew*-jessen, *Hew*-gessen
Huish	*Hew*-ish
Humphrey	*Hum*-fri
Hunstanton	*Hun*-ston, or as spelt
Hyndman	*Hynd*-man

I

Iddesleigh	*Id*-sli
Ightham	*Y*-tam
Inchiquin	*Inch*-quin
Inge	Ing
Ingelow	*In*-jelow
Ingestre	*In*-gestri
Ingham	*Ing*-am
Inglis	*In*-gools, or as spelt
Innes	*In*-nis
Inveraray	Inver-*air*-i
Inverarity	Inver-*arr*-iti
Isitt	*Y*-sit
Iveagh	*Y*-va

J

Jacoby	*Jack*-obi
Jeaffreson	*Jeff*-erson
Jeffreys	*Jef*-riz
Jerome	Jer-*ōm*
Jervaulx	*Jer*-vis, *Jer*-vō
Jervis	*Jar*-vis, *Jer*-vis
Jervois	*Jar*-vis
Jeune	Jōōn
Jeyes	Jays
Jocelyn	*Joss*-lin
Jolliffe	*Joll*-if
Julyan	*Jōō*-lian

K

Kaberry	*Kay*-berry
Keatinge	*Keet*-ing
Keighley	*Keeth*-li
Keightley	*Keet*-li
Keiller	*Kee*-ler
Kekewich	*Keck*-wich
Kennard	Ken-ard
Kenyon	*Ken*-yon
Keogh, Keough, Kehoe	*Kee*-ō
Kesteven	*Kest*-even
Kaynes, Keynes	Keens
Killanin	Kill-*an*-in
Kilmorey	Kil-*mur*-ri
Kincairney	Kin-*cair*-ni
Kingscote	*Kings*-cut
Kinnaird	Kin-*naird*
Kinnear	Kin-*near*
Kinnoull	Kin-*nōōl*
Kirkcudbright	Kirk-*oo*-bri
Knightly	*Nyt*-ly
Knighton	*Ny*-ton

Knollys, Knowles	Nōlz
Knutsford	*Nuts*-ford
Kynaston	*Kin*-naston

L

Lacon	*Lay*-kon
Laffan	La-*ffan*
Langrishe	*Lang*-rish
Larpent	*Lar*-pent
Lascelles	*Las*-sels
Lathom	*Lay*-thom
Laughton	*Law*-ton
Lavengro	*Lav*-engrō
Lawrence	*Lor*-rence
Layard	Laird, or as spelt
Lea	Lee
Learmonth	*Ler*-munth
Leatham	*Leeth*-am
Leathes	Leeths, *Leeth*-iz
Lechmere	*Leech*-meer
Leconfield	*Lek*-onfield
Le Fanu	*Leff*-enyōō, *Leff*-nōō
Lefevre	Le-*fee*-ver
Lefroy	Le-*froy*
Legard	*Lej*-ard
Legge	Leg
Legh	Lee
Lehmann	*Lay*-man
Leicester	*Lest*-er
Leigh	Lee
Leighton	*Lay*-ton
Leinster	Len-ster, *Lin*-ster
Leishman	*Leesh*-man
Leitrim	*Leet*-rim
Lemesurier	Le-*mézu*rer
Leominster	*Lem*-ster
Le Patourel	Le-*pat*-turel

Le Poer	Le *Por*
Le Queux	Le *Kew*
Leven	*Lee*-ven
Leverhulme	*Lee*-verhewm
Leveson-Gower	*Lōō*-son-Gaw
Levey	*Lee*-vi, *Lev*-vi
Ley	Lee
Leyland	*Lay*-land
Liardet	*Lee*-ardet
Lingen	*Ling*-en
Lisle	Lyle, Leel
Listowel	Lis-*tō*-el
Llangattock	Klan-*gat*-tock
Llewellyn	Loo-*ell*-in
Lochiel	Lok-*heel*
Logue	Lōg
Lough	Luff
Loughborough	*Luf*-burra
Lovat	*Luv*-at
Lovibond	*Luv*-band, also as spelt
Lowther	*Low*-ther
Lugard	Lōō-*gard*
Lygon	*Lig*-gon
Lymington	*Lim*-mington
Lympne	Lim
Lynam	*Ly*-nam
Lysaght	*Ly*-sat or *Ly*-sacht
Lysons	*Ly*-sons
Lyveden	*Liv*-den

M

Macalister	Mac-*al*-ister
Macara	Mac-*ah*-ra
McCorquodale	Ma-*cork*-odale
Maccullagh	Ma-*cul*-la
M'Culloch	Ma-*cul*-lokh
M'Eachern	Mac-*kek*-run

McEvoy	*Mack*-evoy
M'Ewan, MacEwen	Mac-*kew*-an
M'Gee, M'Ghee	Ma-*gee*
MacGillivray	Ma-*gil*-vri, Ma-*gili*-vray
M'Gillycuddy	*Mack*-licuddi
Machell	*May*-chell
Machen	*May*-chen
M'Illwraith	*Mack*-ilrayth
MacIver, M'Ivor	Mac-*ky*-ver
McKay	Mac-*ky*
Mackie	*Mack*-i
Maclachlan	Mac-*laukh*-lan
Maclagan	Mac-*lag*-gan
Maclaren	Mac-*lar*-ren
Maclean	Ma-*clayn*
Macleay	Ma-*clay*
Macleod	Ma-*clowd*
Macmahon	Mac-*mahn* (with internal h)
Macnamara	Macna-*mah*-ra
M'Naught	Mac-*nawt*
MacNaughton	Mac-*naw*-ton
Macneill	Mac-*neel*
Maconchy	Ma-*conk*-i
Maconochie	Mack-*on*-okhi
Magdalen(e)	*Mawd*-lin
Magrath	Ma-*grah*
Maguire	Ma-*gwire*
Mahon	Mahn, Ma-*hoon*
Mahony	*Mah*-ni, Ma-*hōn*-i
Mainwaring	*Man*-nering
Majendie	*Maj*-endi
Malet	*Mal*-let
Mall, The	Mal, The
Malmesbury	*Mahm*-sbri
Mansergh	*Man*-zer
Marjoribanks	*March*-banks
Marlborough	*Mawl*-bra
Martineau	*Mart*-inō

Masham	*Mass*-am
Maskelyne	*Mask*-elin
Massereena	Mazereena
Mather	*May*-ther, *Math*-er
Matheson	*Math*-ison, *Mat*-tison
Maugham	Mawm
Maughan	Mawn
Maunsell	*Man*-sell
Maurice	*Mor*-ris
Mayo	*May*-ō
Meath	Meeth
Meiklejohn	*Mick*-eljon
Meldrum	*Mel*-drum
Melhuish	*Mel*-lish
Menzies	*Meng*-iz, *Menz*-iz, *Ming*-iz
Meopham	*Mep*-am, *Meff*-am
Mereworth	*Merri*-worth
Meux	Mewz
Meyer	*My*-er
Meynell	*Men*-nel
Meyrick	*Mer*-rick
Meysey-Thompson	*May*-zi-*Toms*-on
Michelham	*Mich*-lam
Michie	*Mik*-ki
Midleton	Middleton
Mildmay	*Myld*-may
Millard	Mil-*lard*
Milles	Mills
Milngavie	Mull-*gy*
Molyneaux, Molyneux	*Molli*-nō, *Molli*-new
Monaghan	*Mon*-nahan
Monck	Munk
Monckton	*Munk*-ton
Moncrieff	Mon-*creef*
Monkhouse	*Munk*-hows
Monkswell	*Munk*-swell
Monro, Monroe	Mun-*rō*
Monson	*Mun*-son

Montagu	*Mont*-agew
Monteagle	Mun-*tee*-gle
Montefiore	Montifi-*or*-i
Montgomery	Munt-*gum*-meri
Monzie	Mun-*ee*
Moran	*Mor*-an
Morant	Mo-*rant*
Moray	*Mur*-ri
Mordaunt	*Mor*-dunt
Morice	*Mo*-rris
Morrell	Murr-*ell*
Mostyn	*Moss*-tin
Mouat	*Moo*-at
Moule	Mōl
Moulton	*Mōl*-ton
Mountmorres	Mount-*mor*-ris
Mowat	*Mō*-at, *Moo*-at
Mowbray	*Mow*-bri, *Mōō*-bri
Moynihan	*Moy*-ni-han
Muncaster	*Mun*-kaster

N

Naas	Nace
Naesmyth	*Nay*-smith
Napier	*Nay*-pier
Neave	Neev
Neil	Neel
Nepean	Ne-*peen*
Newburgh	*New*-bra
Newnes	Newns
Nigel	*Ny*-jel
Niven	*Niv*-ven
Northbourne	*North*-burn
Northcote	*North*-cot
Nunburnholme	Nun-*bern*-um

O

O'Callaghan	Ō-*call*-ahan
Ochterlony	Octerl-*o*-ni
O'Donoghue	Ō-*dun*-nah
Ogilvy	Ō-gelvi
O'Hagan	Ō-*hay*-gan
Olivier	O-*liv*-vier, O-*liv*-iay
O'Meara	Ō-*mah*-ra
O'Morchoe	Ō-*mur*-roo
Onions	Ō-*ny*-ons, *Un*-ions
Ormonde	*Or*-mond
Osbourne	*Os*-burn, *Os*-born
O'Shaughnessy	Ō-*shaw*-nessi, Ō-*shawk*-nessi
Outram	*Ōō*tram

P

Paget	*Paj*-it
Pakenham	*Pack*-enum
Palgrave	*Pal*-grave
Parnell	*Par*-nal
Pasley	*Pay*-zli
Paterson	*Pat*-terson
Paton	*Pay*-ton
Pauncefote	*Powns*-foot
Pease	Peez
Pechell	*Pee*-chel
Pembroke	*Pem*-brook
Pennefather	*Pen*-nifether
Pennycuick	*Pen*-nicook, *Pen*-niquick
Penrhyn	Pen-*rin*
Pepys	Peeps (ancient), *Pep*-piss (modern)
Pery	*Peer*-i
Peto	*Pee*-tō
Petre	*Pee*-ter
Petrie	*Pee*-tri
Pierpoint, Pierrepoint	*Peer*-pont, also as spelt

Pigou	Pi-*goo*
Pirbright	*Per*-brite
Pirie	Pirri
Pleydell-Bouverie	*Pled*-el *Bōō*-veri
Pochin	*Putch*-in
Pole	Pōōl, Pōl
Pole Carew	Pool *Cair*-i
Poltimore	*Pol*-timor
Polwarth	*Pōl*-werth
Ponsonby	*Pun*-sunbi
Pontefract	*Pum*-fret, also as spelt
Portal	*Por*-tal
Porteous	*Por*-tius
Poulett	*Pau*-let
Powell	*Pō*-ell, *Pow*-ell
Powerscourt	*Poor*-scort
Powlett	*Paw*-let
Powys	*Pō*-is
Praed	Prade
Pretyman	*Prit*-timan
Prevost	*Prev*-vō
Prideaux	*Pree*-dō, *Prid*-dux, *Prid*-dō
Probyn	*Pro*-bin
Prothero	*Proth*-erō
Prowse	Prowz
Pugh	Pew
Pwellheli	*Pōōl*-helli
Pytchley	*Pych*-li

R

Ralegh	*Raw*-li, *Ral*-li
Ralph	Ralf, Rafe
Ranelagh	*Ran*-ela
Ranfurly	*Ran*-ferli
Ranjitsinhji	*Ran*-jit-*sin*-ji
Rankeillour	Rankiller
Rashleigh	*Rash*-li

Rathdonnell	Rath-*don*-nel
Rathmore	Rath-*mor*
Rayleigh	*Ray*-li
Raynham	*Rain*-am
Reading	*Red*-ing
Reay	Ray
Renwick	*Ren*-nick
Reuter	*Roy*-ter
Rhondda	*Ron*-tha
Rhys	Rees, Rice
Riddell	*Rid*-dle
Rievaulx	Riv-els, *Reev*-ō
Robartes	Ro-*barts*
Roche	Rōch
Rolleston	*Rol*-ston
Romilly	*Rom*-ili
Romney	*Rum*-ni, *Rom*-ni
Ronaldshay	*Ron*-ald-shay
Rothes	*Roth*-is
Rothwell	*Row*-ell, also as spelt
Rouse	Rouse
Routh	Rowth
Roxburghe	*Rox*-bra
Ruislip	*Ry*-slip
Ruthven	*Riv*-ven, *Ri*-then

S

Sacheverell	Sash-*ev*-erel
St Aubyn	S'nt *Aw*-bin
St Clair	*Sin*-clair
St Cyres	Sin-*seer*
St John	*Sin*-jun
St Leger	*Sil*-linjer, S'nt *Lej*-er
St Maur	S'nt *Mōr*, *See*-mer
St Neots	S'nt *Neets*
Salisbury	*Sawl*-sberri
Saltoun	*Sawl*-ton, *Sal*-ton

Sandes, Sandys	Sands
Sault-St Marie	*Soo*-St Marie
Saumarez, Sausmarez	*So*-marrez, *Sum*-mers
Saunders	*Sahn*-ders, *Sawn*-ders
Saunderson	*Sahn*-derson, *Sawn*-derson
Saye and Sele	Say an Seel
Sayer	Sair, also as spelt
Scafell	*Scaw*-fell, *Scah*-fell
Scarborough	*Scar*-burra
Scarbrough	*Scar*-bra
Sclater	*Slay*-ter
Scone	Scōōn
Scrymgeour	*Scrim*-jer
Searle	Serl
Sedbergh	*Sed*-ber
Sempill	*Semp*-il
Sergeant	*Sar*-jent
Seton, Setoun	*See*-ton
Seymour	*See*-mer, *See*-mor
Shakerley	*Shak*-erli
Shearman	*Sher*-man
Sherborne	*Sher*-bern, *Sher*-born
Shrewsbury	*Shrō*-sberri, (town) also *Shrōō*-sberri
Sidebotham	*Side*-bottam
Skrine	Skreen
Slaithwaite	*Slō*-it, also as spelt
Smijth	Smyth
Sodor	*Sō*-dor
Somers	*Sum*-mers
Somerset	*Sum*-erset
Somerton	*Sum*-merton
Sondes	Sonds
Sotherby	*Suth*-ebi
Southwell	*Su*-thell
Speight	Spate
Stalbridge	*Stawl*-bridge
Stanton	*Stahn*-ton
Stavordale	*Stay*-vordale

Stormonth	*Stor*-munth
Stoughton	*Staw*-ton, *Stow*-ton
Stourton	*Ster*-ton
Strachan	*Strack*-en
Strachey	*Stray*-chi
Strahan	Strawn
Stranraer	Stran-*rar*
Strathallan	Strath-*al*-an
Strathcona	Strath-*cō*-na
Stratheden	Strath-*ee*-den
Strathmore	*Strath*-mor
Stucley	*Stew*-kli
Sudeley	*Sewd*-li
Sudley	*Sud*-li
Suirdale	*Sheur*-dale
Sweatman	*Swet*-man
Sweetman	*Sweet*-man
Symonds	*Sim*-monds
Symons	*Sim*-mons, also as spelt
Synge	Sing

T

Tangye	*Tang*-i
Teignmouth	*Tin*-muth
Tewkesbury	*Tewks*-berri
Teynham	*Tan*-am
Thames	Tems
Theobald	*Tib*-bald, also as spelt
Thesiger	*Thes*-sijer
Thorold	*Thur*-uld, also as spelt
Thuillier	*Twil*-lier
Thynne	Thin
Tighe	Ty
Tollemache	*Tol*-mash
Torphichen	Tor-*fick*-en
Toynbee	*Toyn*-bi
Trafalgar	Tra-*fal*-gar (Square), Trafal-*gar* (title)

Traquair	Trak-*ware*
Tredegar	Tred-*ee*-gar
Trefusis	Tre-*few*-sis
Treloar	Tre-*lor*
Trevelyan	Tre-*vi*-lian
Trewin	Tre-*win*
Trimlestown	*Trim*-melston
Troubridge	*Trōō*-bridge
Tuite	Tewt
Tullibardine	Tulli-*bard*-een
Turnour	*Ter*-ner
Tyrwhitt	*Tir*-rit
Tyssen	*Ty*-sen
Tytler	*Tyt*-ler

U

Uist	*Ōō*-ist
Urquhart	*Erk*-ert
Uttoxeter	Yōō-*tox*-eter

V

Vanburgh	*Van*-bra
Van Dyck	Van-*dyke*
Van Straubenzee	Van Straw-*ben*-zie
Vaughan	Vawn
Vaux	Voks, Vōks
Vavasour	*Vav*-vaser
Vesey	*Vee*-zi
Villiers	*Vil*-lers
Vyvyan	*Viv*-vian

W

Waldegrave	*Wawl*-grave
Waleran	*Wawl*-ran

Walford	*Wawl*-ford
Wallop	*Wol*-lup
Walmesley	*Wawm*-sli
Walsingham	*Wawl*-singam
Wantage	*Won*-tij
Warburton	*War*-burton
Warre	Wor
Warwick	*Wor*-rick
Wauchope	*Waw*-kup
Waugh	Waw
Wednesbury	*Wens*-berri
Weir	Weer
Wellesley	*Wel*-sli, *Wes*-li
Wemyss	Weems
Westcott	*West*-cot
Westenra	*West*-enra
Whalley	*Whay*-li
Wilde	Wyld
Willard	Will-*ard*
Willes	Wills
Willoughby	*Wil*-lobi
Willoughby-D'Eresby	*Wil*-lobi-Dersbi
Willoughby de Broke	*Wil*-loby de Brook
Winchilsea	*Winch*-elsee
Winstanley	*Win*-stanli
Woburn	*Wōō*-bern
Wodehouse	*Wood*-house
Wolcombe	*Wool*-cum
Wollaston	*Wool*-aston
Wolmer	*Wool*-mer
Wolseley	*Wool*-sli
Wombwell	*Woom*-well
Woolwich	*Wool*-ich
Worcester	*Woos*-ter
Worsley	*Wer*-sli
Wortley	*Wert*-li
Wraxhall	*Rax*-all
Wreford	*Ree*-ford

Wrey	Ray
Wriothesley	*Ry*-othsli, *Rox*-li
Wrixon	*Rix*-on
Wrotham	*Rōō*-tham, *Rōō*-tem
Wrottesley	*Rot*-sli
Wroughton	*Raw*-ton
Wylie, Wyllie	*Wy*-li

Y and Z

Yeates	Yayts
Yeatman	*Yayt*-man
Yeats	Yayts
Yerburgh	*Yar*-burra
Yonge	Yung
Zouche	Zōōsh

ORDER OF PRECEDENCE

Certain categories of people due to who they are (members of the royal family, peers and knights) or what office they hold (officers of state, judges) are ranked in an order of precedence. The list can be used when deciding the order in which guests arrive at official functions and ceremonies and for seating plans. The rules are based on custom and on statutes.

Women take the same order of precedence as their husbands. Peeresses in their own right take the same precedence as peers of the same rank.

The Table of Precedence in England and Wales

The Sovereign
The Duke of Edinburgh
The Heir Apparent (The Prince of Wales)
The Sovereign's younger sons
The Sovereign's grandsons
The Sovereign's cousins
Archbishop of Canterbury
Lord High Chancellor
Archbishop of York
Prime Minister
Lord President of the Council
Speaker of the House of Commons
Speaker of the House of Lords
President of the Supreme Court
Lord Chief Justice of England and Wales
Lord Privy Seal
Ambassadors and High Commissioners
Lord Great Chamberlain
Earl Marshal
Lord Steward of the Household
Lord Chamberlain of the Household
Master of the Horse
Dukes of England
Dukes of Scotland
Dukes of Great Britain
Dukes of Ireland
Dukes of UK and Ireland since the Union
Eldest sons of Dukes of the Blood Royal
Ministers, Envoys, and other important overseas visitors

Marquesses of England
Marquesses of Scotland
Marquesses of Great Britain
Marquesses of Ireland
Marquesses of UK and Ireland since the Union
Eldest sons of Dukes
Earls of England
Earls of Scotland
Earls of Great Britain
Earls of Ireland
Earls of UK and Ireland since the Union
Younger sons of Dukes of the Blood Royal
Eldest sons of Marquesses
Younger sons of Dukes
Viscounts of England
Viscounts of Scotland
Viscounts of Great Britain
Viscounts of Ireland
Viscounts of UK and Ireland since the Union
Eldest sons of Earls
Younger sons of Marquesses
Bishop of London
Bishop of Durham
Bishop of Winchester
Other English Diocesan Bishops according to seniority of consecration
Retired Church of England Diocesan Bishops according to seniority of
    consecration
Suffragan Bishops according to seniority of consecration
Secretaries of State if a Baron
Barons of England
Lords of Parliament, Scotland
Barons of Great Britain
Barons of Ireland
Barons of UK and Ireland since the Union, including Life Barons
Master of the Rolls
Deputy President of the Supreme Court
Justices of the Supreme Court, according to seniority of appointment
Lords Commissioners of the Great Seal (when existing)
Treasurer of the Household
Comptroller of the Household
Vice-Chamberlain of the Household

Secretaries of State, under the rank of Baron
Eldest sons of Viscounts
Younger sons of Earls
Eldest sons of Barons
Knights of the Garter
Privy Counsellors
Chancellor of the Order of the Garter
Chancellor of the Exchequer
Chancellor of the Duchy of Lancaster
President of the Queen's Bench Division
President of the Family Division
Chancellor of the High Court
Lord Justices of Appeal according to seniority of appointment
Judges of High Court according to seniority of appointment
Younger sons of Viscounts
Younger sons of Barons
Sons of Life Peers
Baronets, according to date of Patent
Knights of the Thistle
Knights Grand Cross of the Order of the Bath
Knights Grand Commander of the Order of St Michael and St George
Knights Grand Cross of the Royal Victorian Order
Knights Grand Cross of the Order of the British Empire
Knights Commander of the Order of the Bath
Knights Commander of the Order of St Michael and St George
Knights Commander of the Royal Victorian Order
Knights Commander of the Order of the British Empire
Knights Bachelor
Circuit Judges in England and Wales
Master of the Court of Protection
Companions of the Order of the Bath
Companions of the Order of St Michael and St George
Commanders of the Royal Victorian Order
Commanders of the Order of the British Empire
Companions of the Distinguished Service Order
Lieutenants of the Royal Victorian Order
Officers of the Order of the British Empire
Companions of the Imperial Service Order
Eldest sons of the younger sons of peers
Eldest sons of baronets
Eldest sons of knights according to the precedence of their fathers

Members of the Royal Victorian Order
Members of the Order of the British Empire
Younger sons of baronets
Younger sons of knights according to the precedence of their fathers

The Table of Precedence in Scotland

The Sovereign
The Duke of Edinburgh
Lord High Commissioner to the General Assembly of the Church of
 Scotland (while that assembly is sitting)
Duke of Rothesay (eldest son of the Sovereign)
The Sovereign's younger sons
The Sovereign's grandsons
The Sovereign's nephews
Lord-Lieutenants
Lord Provosts
Sheriffs Principal
Lord Chancellor of Great Britain
Moderator of the General Assembly of the Church of Scotland
Keeper of the Great Seal of Scotland (the First Minister)
Presiding Officer
Secretary of State for Scotland
Hereditary High Constable of Scotland
Hereditary Master of the Household in Scotland
Dukes, as in England
Eldest sons of Dukes of the Blood Royal
Marquesses, as in England
Eldest sons of Dukes
Earls, as in England
Younger sons of Dukes of the Blood Royal
Eldest sons of Marquesses
Younger sons of Dukes
Lord Justice-General
Lord Clerk Register
Lord Advocate
Advocate General
Lord Justice-Clerk
Viscounts, as in England
Eldest sons of Earls
Younger sons of Marquesses
Barons or Lords of Parliament (Scotland), as in England

Eldest sons of Viscounts
Younger sons of Earls
Eldest sons of Barons or Lords of Parliament
Knights of the Garter
Knights of the Thistle
Privy Counsellors
Senators of the College of Justice (Lords of Session)
Younger sons of Viscounts
Younger sons of Barons or Lords of Parliament
Baronets
Knights Grand Cross of Orders, as in England
Knights Commanders of Orders, as in England
Solicitor-General for Scotland
Lord Lyon King of Arms
Sheriffs Principal
Knights Bachelor
Sheriffs
Companions of the Order of the Bath
Companions of the Order of St Michael and St George
Commanders of the Royal Victorian Order
Commanders of the Order of the British Empire
Companions of the Distinguished Service Order
Lieutenants of the Royal Victorian Order
Officers of the Order of the British Empire
Companions of the Imperial Service Order
Eldest sons of the younger sons of peers
Eldest sons of baronets
Eldest sons of knights according to the precedence of their fathers
Members of the Royal Victorian Order
Members of the Order of the British Empire
Younger sons of baronets
Younger sons of knights according to the precedence of their fathers

Index

A